Praise for

MOTHERCARE

A *Slate* Best Book of the Year

"The book's great service is to disentangle love from care, or at least complicate their relationship—a radical proposition for women especially . . . As Tillman shows, caregiving is not intrinsically virtuous, a sacred act to be reified; sometimes it is simply necessity." —KATE WOLF, *n+1*

"*MOTHERCARE* represents an investigation of the question of duty, or conscience, what we owe or want to provide to the people in our lives . . . For a reader, there's something bracing about Tillman's honesty, which transforms *MOTHER-CARE* from a record or a logbook into a work of art."
—DAVID ULIN, *Los Angeles Times*

"Electrifying." —*Vulture*, a Best Book of the Year

"Unflinching . . . It offers an unsparing account of the American health-care system and a starkly unsentimental portrait of the mechanics of looking after a person who is dying very slowly. Drawing on skills she's honed as a novelist and cultural critic, she crafts an account at once formally restrained and emotionally weighty . . . An urgent piece of nonfiction."
—MEGHAN O'ROURKE, *Bookforum*

"Tillman captures such complexities around the human condition without sentimentality and, as always, makes vital our deepest flaws—she is as unsparing of her mother as she is herself, and is incredibly frank about loving and living with a difficult parent. Realistic and imbued with her familiar candour, I'm grateful for the strength and presence she packs on the page."   —ANNA CAFOLLA, *The Face*

"Lynne Tillman's work always feels fresh and insightful."
                                        —*Vol. 1 Brooklyn*

"Tillman has in this slim memoir of the final years of her mother's life zeroed in on an underrepresented facet of the universal contract: our queasy anxiety that the relationship might, in the end, be transactional . . . *MOTHERCARE* is practical, not sentimental. It flirts with being analytical. It's even useful, as Tillman runs through her and her sisters' travails dealing with doctors and home care. Though it is memoir and not a novel, only Tillman the novelist could have produced it."
—JEREMY M. DAVIES, *The New York Times Book Review*

"This is a well written, memorably unsentimental account of one family's medical struggles and the ill feelings they released. Tillman's goal was to tell a 'cautionary tale' that 'may be helpful, informative, consoling, or upsetting.' She was right on all counts." —MICHAEL MAGRAS, *Star Tribune* (Minneapolis)

"*MOTHERCARE* forces us to question our assumptions about what is owed to us and about our responsibility to our family members . . . So many of the revelations of this book—and indeed the predicament that we find ourselves in when caring for others—come down to, as Tillman puts it, learning what we never wanted to know. But it seems unlikely that conditions will improve unless we approach the crisis, as Tillman has done in this book, with unsparing honesty." —JESSICA FERRI, *Los Angeles Times*

"A masterfully-wrought story of ambivalence that is both heartbreaking and exasperating . . . [A] stunning story of caregiving." —ELISSA ALTMAN, *The Boston Globe*

"As Tillman expresses at the outset, each story of caregiving will be defined by the particulars: the medical conditions, the geography, the insurance, the budget, and the people involved, with their pasts and predispositions. Caring for her mother showed Tillman how much she herself had wanted to be cared for, how hard it is to share the burden with anyone else . . . Caring reveals, too, the threadbare nature of the support networks we have to cobble together when, predictably, inevitably, someone needs care; in this country, family obligations remain intensely personal. It is the reason, perhaps, why these common problems remain so uncommonly discussed."

—ANNA ALTMAN, *The New Republic*

"Discerning . . . Tillman's frank insights on love and loss are cannily original."   —*Publishers Weekly*

"An unsparing and heart-wrenching exploration of serious illness and its impact on everyone it touches."
                    —*Kirkus Reviews* (starred review)

"*MOTHERCARE* is a close examination of the American health-care system, the constraints of family, and the complexities of care. Tillman's writing is devastating—unsentimental, honest, full of sharp intelligence and irrepressible wit. *MOTHERCARE* resonates."
                    —KATIE KITAMURA, author of *Intimacies*

"We know Lynne Tillman as a brilliant stylist in the first person, but she has never written a work as intimate and frank as *MOTHERCARE*. This philosophical memoir deepens my admiration for her inimitable sentences, drawing me confidently and calmly into contemplation of two universal, terrifying, awe-inspiring, ever-intertwined themes: death and moms."   —LUCY IVES, author of *Cosmogony*

"*MOTHERCARE* is written with lucid, beautifully crafted prose. As in her novels, Tillman makes the ineffable a plain fact through her craft, by defying genres and presenting us with a text that's impossible to put down despite its difficult subject. This book is a gift that may or may not help caregivers, the grieving, and the dying—but it will certainly do no harm as it honors the fundamental commitment of an ideal physician." —GREGG BORDOWITZ, author of *Some Styles of Masculinity*

"Lynne Tillman's terrifying, fascinating memoir shows how it is, the intimacy of mother-daughter connection at the ending, close-up, yet playing out within the larger world of race and class. *MOTHERCARE* is really really real!" —NELL PAINTER, author of *Old in Art School: A Memoir of Starting Over*

"A touching, heartfelt guide for the care of an ailing parent in need of compassion and lifesaving medical assistance. In an era when modern medicine is fast-paced, patient advocacy is essential, not only so that our loved ones receive the best possible care, but also that it respects their dignity." —DR. VIJAY VAD, author of *Back Rx* and sports medicine specialist at the Hospital for Special Surgery, New York

ALSO BY LYNNE TILLMAN

NOVELS

Haunted Houses (1987)

Motion Sickness (1991)

Cast in Doubt (1992)

No Lease on Life (1998)

American Genius, A Comedy (2006)

Men and Apparitions (2018)

SHORT STORY COLLECTIONS

Absence Makes the Heart (1990)

The Madame Realism Complex (1992)

This Is Not It (2002)

Someday This Will Be Funny (2011)

Weird Fucks (2015)

The Complete Madame Realism and Other Stories (2016)

NONFICTION

The Velvet Years: Warhol's Factory 1965–67 (1995)

The Broad Picture: Essays 1987–1996 (1997)

Bookstore: The Life and Times of Jeannette Watson and Books & Co. (1999)

What Would Lynne Tillman Do? (2014)

MOTHERCARE

An Autobiographical Essay

LYNNE
TILLMAN

Soft Skull  New York

First Soft Skull edition: 2022
First paperback edition: 2023

Grateful acknowledgment for reprinting materials is made to the following: Laurie Simmons, *Woman/Heels (Floating on Back)*, from the series *Family Collision*. Courtesy of Laurie Simmons © 1981. "Pasteur Pharmacy" photograph © 2014 by Robby Virus. Information on page 24 was retrieved from www.nph.org.

The Library of Congress has cataloged the hardcover edition as follows:
Names: Tillman, Lynne, author.
Title: Mothercare : an autobiographical essay / Lynne Tillman.
Description: First Soft Skull edition. | New York : Soft Skull, 2022.
Identifiers: LCCN 2021052255 | ISBN 9781593767174 (hardcover) | ISBN 9781593767181 (ebook)
Subjects: LCSH: Tillman, Lynne. | Tillman, Lynne—Family. | Hydrocephalus—Patients—Family relationships. | Women caregivers—United States—Biography. | Adult children of aging parents—United States—Biography. | Parent and adult child—United States.
Classification: LCC RC391 .T55 2022 | DDC 616.85/88430092 [B]—dc23/eng/20220228
LC record available at https://lccn.loc.gov/2021052255

Paperback ISBN: 978-1-59376-762-4

Cover design by Nicole Caputo
Book design by Wah-Ming Chang

Published by Soft Skull Press
New York, NY
www.softskull.com

Printed in the United States of America

1 3 5 7 9 10 8 6 4 2

To caregivers,
paid and unpaid

Ducunt volentem fata, nolentem trahunt.

The fates lead him who will, drag him who will not.

MOTHERCARE

I once embedded dreams in stories, then lost faith in their meanings for anyone but me. Lately, a messy house has shown up in them. Mother kept an orderly house, nothing out of place, furniture dusted, carpets vacuumed, wood floors waxed, no clutter except in my bedroom. I didn't put everything away, clothes, books, and didn't care until she saw it. Mother became enraged by my messy dresser drawers, and occasionally dumped them out onto the floor. That infuriated me. The messy house dream appears, it repeats like disorderly thoughts. Not everything can be put away.

In late 1994, Mother became ill. For about eleven years, she was dependent on her three daughters, my two sisters and me, and on doctors, companions, aides, physical therapists, and other professionals. She remained at home in her Manhattan apartment with a full-time caregiver. My sisters and I shared in her upkeep, deciding medical issues, and maintaining her in a comfortable home. Keeping her alive was done generously, but not selflessly, and also as a grueling obligation. Those eleven years were frustrating, an education, oddly enlightening, let's say, they were morbidly enlightened. Those years were maddening and depressing. And I learned what I never wanted to know.

To adult children who care for sick parents, this story will be familiar, with variations, since the problems are the same and also different. To adult children who have not yet needed to care for their parents, or may never, lucky dogs, this may be a cautionary tale.

Other families will tell other stories and will have had stranger experiences. My sisters would tell different versions of the same events and relate other events. Any incident is filtered subjectively, which causes memoirs and oral histories to be compelling as much for their versions of honesty, what they remember, the facts of their lives, as for their untrustworthiness, misinformation, and bias.

Ironically, I once wrote: "Experience teaches not to trust experience," and that's true, certainly someone else's should be suspect. And what people gain from their own experience is not necessarily helpful to them.

Sometimes I felt a kind of benignity in caring for Mother, sometimes hopelessness and fury.

Writing this cautionary tale, I expect some recognition and some resemblances to others' experiences, but there will be many small and large differences. Most critically, there will be the matter of point of view, the magistrate of narratives. Whether fiction or nonfiction, any story or account represents the storyteller's.

This is a partial picture, told from my vantage point, and possibly to my advantage, though I hope to write against that tendency. My object: To tell you a story that may be helpful, informative, consoling, or upsetting. I want to say about this situation: It is impossible to get it completely right.

Sophie Merrill was born on Ludlow Street, March 30, 1908, and grew up on Norfolk Street on the Lower East Side of Manhattan. Her building is still there.

She was a city girl, well educated in public schools, her grammar perfect lifelong—first-generation NYC children of immigrants were drilled in English: she never said "between you and I." In photographs of Sophie with her friends, she looked happy, an attractive, energetic young person— horseback riding, playing tennis, roughhousing on the beach. She had very long hair and an ever-present smile. In portraits, she strikes a serious pose and presents an assured image. Sophie Merrill is always fashionably dressed, often wears a cloche hat, or lets her long dark hair flow freely down her back.

Like my father, Mother attended CCNY night school for two years—it's where they met. Then the worst of the Depression hit, and they dropped out. My father had been taking six courses at night.

My parents had a seven-year courtship, interrupted by one year when they broke up and didn't see each other. His younger brother, Al, told me my father cried into his pillow every night. My father's mother—Russian, beautiful, mad— didn't want him to marry her, or anyone, probably. He was her favorite. But finally they married and had three children over nine years. My sisters are nine and six years older than I, the oldest lives in Manhattan, the middle sister in North Carolina. My parents were a contentious, argumentative couple, I rarely saw affection between them. Their marriage didn't end in divorce, but then, they were old school.

Mother was a smart, resourceful, attractive, tactless, competitive, and practical person. She was what was called a girl with promise, and if times were different, she might have fulfilled that promise. She had wanted to write and paint, but instead she married and had children. She worked for a while before marriage but as soon as my father was making good money, as they called it, she quit, fulfilling an American 1950s ideal— women whose husbands do well will stay at home with their children, content to be wives and mothers. Mother was not, and she was angry, and for that I don't blame her.

When many Americans in the postwar period moved to the suburbs, my parents did also, from the family's comfortable apartment in Brooklyn to a house on Long Island, one partly of their own design. It's where I grew up from the age of five. Mother hadn't wanted to move to the suburbs, but my father insisted on the American dream. It was, in my opinion, a nightmare for Sophie the city girl used to speed, museums, parks, taxis, subways—she didn't like having to drive—and sidewalks, which our street didn't have, ever. It was all forest with a swamp at the end of it.

My parents retired to Florida, where she had never wanted to live; again, my father insisted. With her husband dead in 1984, Mother, alone in Florida, was miserable and bored, but with the help of my New York sister, about three years after my father died, Mother moved to Manhattan. My sister found a great apartment for her on Second Avenue and Twenty-third Street. It was convenient, central, and, because she didn't need to get anywhere fast, crosstown buses were fine.

Her daytime doorman, Ray, told me that, in her first month, he thought Mother couldn't adjust to city life. He thought it would be too hard for her. After another month, Ray said she was doing fine, and they developed a sweet friendship. Ray was a very kind man, avuncular with her, though she was years older.

Almost seventy-nine, Mother discovered a new life, became reacquainted with the city, and an old friend—they had met in school when they were twelve years old—watched movies at MOMA, saw plays, and walked everywhere.

Mother was Kazin's walker in the city, she loved walking. In Florida and the suburbs walking was eccentric.

Mother had seven and a half good years as an independent character.

Then, at eighty-six and a half, Mother showed unusual behavior, symptoms of trouble.

I'd been away almost four months, from September to mid-December 1994, as a visiting writer in the English and American Literature department at the University of Sussex, Brighton, England. During those months, we had no contact. I returned in December, and Mother and I met for breakfast at our usual Polish café. I entered, saw Mother seated at our usual table, and approached, but she didn't look up. She was staring vacantly at the tabletop, and didn't greet me. I said, "Hi, Mom, I've been away, aren't you happy to see me?" She glanced up. "Sure," she said, indifferently. Distant, hair disheveled, she appeared out of sorts, even depressed. Mother was not a depressive; for one, she expressed anger frequently. Her affect now was atypical, puzzling.

We walked uptown to her apartment on Twenty-third Street. On the corner of Thirteenth Street and Second Avenue, we passed what appeared to be a homeless man. Mother commented, "He's waiting for someone." Her interpretation was a kind of identification with him or a projection, and unusual from her mouth. Later, I thought: She's waiting for her husband, my father.

That night or the next morning I phoned one of my two older sisters, I forget which one, probably the New York one. She had noticed the change, also.

Out of the blue, Mother was desperately sick, and it happened to our entire, small family. Each day, in the beginning, the first year or two, seemed urgent. How to handle her condition, what was the right course to help her, what could be done differently and better.

I found all of my diaries for those years but not 1995, the first year of her as-yet-unknown condition. Mother's calendar for 1995 had some missing months, March–October, and by November she no longer kept her calendar. I did, or one of my sisters. Later, her longtime caregiver took over, writing in doctors' and other appointments, physical therapy days. I used the diaries to remember. Some events are sharply in focus, scenes manifest in good detail. What people said, also, whole sentences, responses, queries, they return. Most is lost, especially the moments between, the preludes to bigger events or main events, like Mother's surgeries.

First, we noticed that Mother behaved strangely, she was not herself. I can't remember how we took our first steps, moves toward finding out what was wrong. Those decisions are just lost.

We sisters knew Mother needed an accurate diagnosis, urgently. I don't recall who made the first appointment, with whom. Mother had already had an MRI with her longtime internist. He believed her brain looked normal for an aging brain. He thought the ventricles were normally sized.

A first neurologist, to whose office I brought her, was convinced from the same MRI that she had Alzheimer's. I received a phone call from him—he didn't want to tell me in front of Mother, luckily. I was home, sitting in the kitchen, and he pronounced that awful death sentence. Then he said, "But bring her back in six months, and we'll see." That didn't happen.

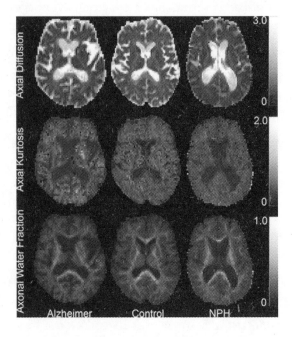

Sample parametric maps for patients with
Alzheimer's disease (*left*), healthy controls (*center*), and
those with normal pressure hydrocephalus (*right*).

Mother's symptoms didn't correlate to a diagnosis of Alzheimer's—the onset of her illness was not incremental; from one day to the next, she showed impairment, her symptoms were not intermittent. She changed significantly or drastically, and the change was consistent.

There were differences among us sisters as time went on. Mother's behavior was erratic and difficult to diagnose, but primarily we stuck to the empirical reality that Mother's condition came on fast, unlike Alzheimer's.

I'm just a medical-science observer, interested in sickness, so-called wellness, cures, trials, placebos, successful and failing bodies. I read medical newsletters, and writers such as Rachel Aviv, Atul Gawande, Siddhartha Mukherjee, and Jane Brody. I read most of the *Times* Science section. Learning that Mother's MRI would be interpreted differently by three of four doctors floored me. Two agreed, the other two differed in their analyses and also from each other. An MRI is not a blueprint; it doesn't tell the brain's secrets.

No certainty in reading the brain and, like reading any text, an MRI requires interpretation, which a doctor decides based on what any one of us brings to any object: education, training, belief, subjectivity. In a sense, perception is immune to objectivity, perception is a disposition: one is disposed to see this way or that, which made finding a conclusive diagnosis for Mother's condition difficult.

Inevitably, patient advocates or family go up against medical experts. In medicine, as in most fields, differences in theory and technique occur. A doctor's expertise is not inviolable. Doctors may even cover uncertainties and inadequacies, their lacks, with clever obfuscation. A patient hopes, expects, that doctors will be honest brokers and admit to their educated guesses, saying: "This may not be the right diagnosis or treatment, but I believe this is what needs to be done." A patient hopes the doctor might, in complicated cases, present several options, expatiating on their advantages and disadvantages. "Of these options, I'd do this," a doctor might say. But patients want to believe there is one best treatment. Often there isn't.

Any opinion or theory provided by the family to the doctor is usually where the doctor starts—analyzing, hypothesizing, speculating, diagnosing. Giving your conclusions first is a mistake. Medical reporting is a narrative, the order of telling influences doctors' first moves and their interpretations. An advocate must be wary of diagnosing symptoms; instead, present evidence or problems chronologically, without interpretation, as best you can. When this happened, what occurred before . . . This isn't easy. Believe me, your empirical observations and impressions matter, but they might not be or shouldn't be answers.

On the other hand, and there are many, passivity hinders. Caregivers might have to get in the doctors' faces, querying their decisions, prescriptions, even annoying them. Doctors are not gods, though some act that way. Some hate being questioned. Some have no time to listen. Some are fine. Many do a good job. They can fire you, I guess, but we never had that experience. More likely, you will need to fire them. Do what you must to get what you need—careful attention, a listener (you also must listen well), genuine thoughtfulness, candor, and truthfulness.

On April 18, 1995, Mother wrote in a stenographer's pad—before my father and she married, she had worked as a secretary and knew stenography:

"Dear Diary, I've been sleeping in my yellow robe for several nights—great comfort even tho one sleeve is drenched to the elbow. Barbara bought a beautiful black bag—I hope she'll be very happy in this purchase. The Japanese restaurant was a delightful place & I liked it a lot. I'm not hungry so I suspect I had more than enough! Enuf! I think I have an ample supply of food for a few days. I'm going to tackle my knitting. My patience is not exhausted yet—No knitting tonight."

"4/19/95 : Breakfast 6:55 AM. I don't know what today has in the offing. I phoned Dr. A (8 AM) expecting a return call. Lynne called. (No Dr. A) . . ."

She wrote that she told my New York sister of her fall-ing-down panty hose. "In heaven's name how can that be since they were under my pantie girdle? . . . So I told the guy at the corner Pasta restaurant, and we had a good laugh—there's nothing like that."

Mother wrote just four short entries in her notepads be-fore stopping. The penultimate began: "Dear Diary, I'm re-ally in a fog not having given a living thought about the rent for this apartment . . ."

Her handwriting, learned well in grammar school, was faint and spidery.

On "Sunday May 1, 1995," she wrote about how, in a dis-cussion with my New York sister, she was "set straight when she let me know I could have driven the car, which by the way we no longer have had one since Nat died nearly ten years ago. I laughed."

The writing is still more uneven and faint, and here Mother makes grammatical errors, which she never did—and, there's a confusion in tenses and a collapsing of time. This is her last entry in this notepad. I find it moving that she mentions her husband "dead nearly ten years."

A friend of my New York sister's recommended his internist, Dr. A. Mother should have a consultation with him, he said. He swore by this doctor.

This was early 1995.

I can visualize Dr. A.'s office and our first visit as if I were looking at a color photograph: The pink-cheeked, youthful-looking, white-haired, bow-tie-wearing doctor is behind a long, wide wooden desk. His is an old-fashioned doctor's office, woody, lived in, and reassuring.

Mother is slumped, in front of his desk, on an old-fashioned fabric club chair. Her body is slipping down, toward the floor. Like a rag doll. Like a child. Like a lost adult.

My New York sister and I are sitting close by and slightly behind Mother.

Dr. A. had examined her privately, and now we are waiting for his crucial judgment.

Dr. A. says, "I'm going to make a subtle diagnosis. I believe your mother has a condition called normal pressure hydrocephalus."

He explained there was too much fluid on her brain, it was not escaping, and the pressure caused specific symptoms: memory loss, frequent urination, a strange gait. She definitely had the first two symptoms, and though Mother's was not exactly the NPH gait, he explained, it was close enough.

NPH was not well known if known at all, and it still isn't. I mention NPH to anyone, even now, the person has never heard of it, 95 percent of the time, and I then define it. In 1995, I had never heard of it. Everything brain-related for the elderly was called dementia, vascular dementia, Alzheimer's, or senility. There seemed to be no other condition. Now, two decades into the twenty-first century, 700,000 people in the United States are supposed to have hydrocephalus, but only 20 percent have been correctly diagnosed.

Mother's condition existed for millennia, but was not named. Its classic symptoms were urinary incontinence, dementia, and gait deviations. Dr. A. recognized her symptoms. We were very, very fortunate.

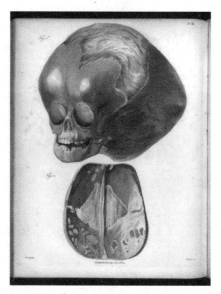

Skull of hydrocephalic child

Dr. A. wasn't a geriatric specialist, but treated many older people—patients age with their doctors. He was sympathetic to them. He was known as a great diagnostician. He looked outside the box, as the saying goes.

Dr. A.'s diagnosis gave Mother a chance: the pressure could be alleviated with a shunt. If the pressure were not checked, she would become a vegetable, he explained. All of her neurological functions would shut down because of the pressure on the brain.

NPH wasn't a hopeless diagnosis like Alzheimer's, but was NPH the right diagnosis. Diagnosis is everything. Dr. A. said we needed to consult a neurologist to be assured it was NPH. He recommended Dr. Z., head of an estimable hospital's neurology department. He thought highly of him.

It was soon apparent to us that Dr. Z. disagreed with Dr. A.'s diagnosis. Dr. Z. didn't say it exactly, he didn't go up against Dr. A. directly, doctors usually don't; but he didn't accept or believe that Mother had NPH. He only obliged and followed her internist's theory—a professional courtesy is what it's called, but courtesy is one of those awful euphemisms. His disbelief affected Mother's recovery, his disbelief made her lose time for her brain to recover.

Dr. Z. saw Mother and did his monthly duties, arrogantly. He performed a spinal tap in his office. I would go into the exam room with them and watch. I had always believed a spinal tap was a horrific procedure, it wasn't. He did it well, swiftly and precisely. I watched several spinal taps—imagine a tap siphoning syrup from a tree—Mother never complained about them, never seemed to experience pain. The tap reduced the buildup of cerebrospinal fluid (CSF) in her brain, and she had minor relief right after them—she became sharper.

Over many months, the neurologist condescended to us and Mother. She had an aging brain or Alzheimer's, and we, her children, weren't accepting reality, the sad truth of Alzheimer's. He quoted Shakespeare in his office, about age and time, while we New York sisters sat there, not challenging him. His arrogance stank. My New York sister was outraged and more indignant than I. We should have fired him, she wanted to, but somehow we felt trapped in the situation. He was Dr. A.'s choice.

Dr. Z.'s negativity affected me, though I thought he was wrong. Still, I found it perplexing, hard not to wonder if he were right, and Mother had no chance. Dr. A. and my New York sister never wavered in their belief it was NPH.

I can't remember an exchange with Dr. A. about Dr. Z. It must have occurred, but if it did, only after fitful months when the pressure on Mother's brain had mounted. We sisters were worried about annoying Dr. A.; this sort of fear never helps a patient who cannot defend herself. It is hard questioning a doctor whom you respect, who is so good, who diagnosed what no other doctor saw or considered. An advocate, as I said, must go up against professionals and experts. They are not only thinking about your charge, they have many.

✦

A doctor's office can be chaotic, your appointment is for 1 p.m., and it's 2:30 p.m. The doctor had an emergency. And people forget, you forget, the doctor does, the chart is wrong, you left out your allergy to sulfur, assistants misplace forms and figuratively misplace patients.

Everything seemed, to me, to happen all at once, both diffuse and collapsing. The tough health issues, lack of surety, the sense of few or no options and possibilities—weighty obstacles can enfeeble you, and intimidation rattles the ability to meet your goals. There is no choice, really, but to work hard to overcome these, to be gutsy.

Life doesn't proceed in an orderly way. It frustrates people who need to control every part of their lives, who go berserk when anything changes on them. Life doesn't allow it, total control, and things will go south, and north, every which unexpected way.

We did have Mother see a different neurosurgeon and neurologist, later.

The best part, if I can say that about Mother's condition, was her passivity, her acquiescence. Her condition let us take charge, choose doctors, make appointments. Mother allowed us to do what was necessary. She might be very confused, might become angry, but ultimately she would do what we told her to do, what she needed to do. Mostly, we went unquestioned.

We sisters had to learn the hard way—many trials, many errors. One trial: Mother's anxiety about time. We had to learn not to tell her about a future appointment or event. If, let's say, she was told she was going to see a doctor tomorrow, while her brain was colloquially confused, she might awaken at 6:00 in the morning. She would demand to be dressed right then. Told the appointment was at 3:30 p.m., and there was lots of time, didn't matter. She wouldn't relent, she wanted to get dressed, and could come close to hysteria, again colloquially, if she wasn't.

Reasoning didn't work; her anxiety was way beyond reason. You must relent, and change your behavior. You placate the anxious person. Still, she would insist to be dressed, and want to leave for the appointment six hours early. All day, until she actually had to leave with her companion, she was miserable and worried. We're going to be late, she'd say. With hours to go, she would drive me crazy.

We adapted, learning to tell her she had an appointment on the morning of it. Then her anxiety didn't build up. Understanding or adjusting to a mind whose thought process is damaged is a matter of sympathy, of acceptance. Adapting to a brain that's damaged is hard; your own reason is strained and tested. I didn't know what Mother was experiencing, what she felt, except that her behavior demonstrated her decreased capacities, and caused her alarm and stress of all kinds. Her own confused mind must have been a hell to her. Her experience of time was distorted.

Einstein wrote that we have time only so that everything doesn't happen at once. I have tried to imagine days without time, calendars, clocks and minutes and hours not there to guide me. Imagining timeless days, days indistinguishable, one into the other, not knowing past from present, might be what Mother felt. It was all one day to her. Being so out of time, unable to plan, not able to maintain her own schedule must have been terrifying. Also a terrific blow to her sense of self. A great wound to her pride.

Mother had always been organized, now she wasn't, she couldn't organize anything. She must not have known herself as herself. Frightening to anyone, but to Mother, who prided herself on being organized, and believed, whether as compensation or defense, that she was right, always, it must have been a condemnation. She had never seemed in doubt about her choices. She told me often enough that she was perfect.

She believed in her reasoning powers, her baseline rationality. Famous in our family: Mother's response to Orson Welles's 1938 radio broadcast "War of the Worlds." My parents were listening along with millions. Earth was being invaded by creatures and machines from outer space. They had landed! It was the End, and many took to their beds; my father's best friend, a high school principal, believed this was it. More babies than usual were born nine months later.

Mother said to her husband, "Turn to another station." Rational, smart—of course, no other station was reporting that Earth was overrun by outer-space creatures.

When the brain doesn't function properly, and you don't know what you're thinking or even if you are thinking, you can no longer trust yourself, and then you must do what you can to make sense of life but not as you once lived it. I perceived Mother's efforts to manage herself, deal with her incapacities. Her notebook was one approach, then she lost the capacity even to try.

I paid Mother's bills, and the home care people; and she never queried me. Mother used to balance her checkbook, writing in it in her flowery, clear script. Adding and subtracting. I never tried to balance hers, I never balanced mine. After a while, Mother believed she had millions and millions of dollars. We didn't tell her otherwise. It made her feel good. She always had what she wanted. Without Medicare, it would have been impossible to give Mother the care we did. Her savings, which could have lasted for her lifetime, would've been savaged, my sisters' and my finances decimated. Medicare paid for her operations; and, with co-pays, also her doctor visits. All of Mother's doctors took Medicare assignments. Still, be prepared: Medicare statements and bills are

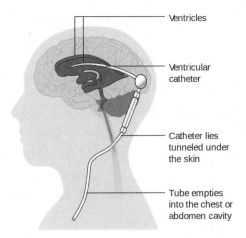

Ventricles

Ventricular
catheter

Catheter lies
tunneled under
the skin

Tube empties
into the chest or
abdomen cavity

Diagram showing a brain shunt

confusing. What has been paid, what hasn't, is hard to figure
out. Luckily, we were helped by a family friend who did that
work professionally.

At last, Drs. Z. and A. agreed that Mother should see a neurosurgeon, whom Dr. A. recommended, even though Dr. Z.
didn't think Mother had NPH.

The neurosurgeon would implant a shunt. The shunt is a
mechanical device that literally shunts CSF from the brain
through a tube under the skin into the stomach. It is like
plumbing under a sink. Many things could go wrong, but we
weren't aware of them. We thought this was Occam's razor.

According to various histories of NPH and the shunt:

— Cases of the disease were described by Hippocrates, Galen, and early and medieval Arabian physicians.

— There weren't any good or reasonably helpful treatments for NPH until, in the late nineteenth century, lumbar punctures were used.

— Today's treatments started in 1949, when the surgeons Frank Nulsen and Eugene Spitz showed that shunts could reduce pressure in the ventricles.

In 1955 a boy was born with Arnold-Chiari malformation (brain tissue extends into the spinal canal) and myelomeningocele (a type of spina bifida). He had Nulsen and Spitz's surgery, but "ventricular taps only temporarily relieved the pressure. All shunt operations, using ventriculoperitoneal shunts constructed with polythene tubing, failed."

John Holter, the boy's father, was a hydraulics technician. He noticed "how the valve in an inter-venous line allowed a needle to be inserted and withdrawn without any leakage of fluid. He explained to Dr. Spitz that "the usage of this type of one-way valve could prevent blockage of the shunt."

He quit his job to develop the shunt, though it was too late to save his son. But it "lacked a material that could be easily sterilized, and wouldn't be rejected by the body . . . Debris and reflux—common in patients who suffer from brain bleeds—could clog the tiny slits."

Intriguing to me, the writer Roald Dahl played a part in the shunt saga. Like Holter, Dahl had a son, but his Theo wasn't born with hydrocephalus. Theo developed it, at age four, after an accident. A Holter shunt was installed, but it clogged and backed up several times. Dahl asked Stanley Wade, a hydraulic engineer who built miniature engines with hydraulic pumps to keep the fuel lines from clogging, to make a device using these hydraulic pumps. Theo's neurosurgeon, Kenneth Till, supervised their efforts. The Wade-Dahl-Till valve helped an estimated three thousand patients recover from secondary hydrocephalus.

Both Dahl and Holter had children with hydrocephalus, a strong motivation to find a cure, a necessity close to the heart.

A boy in my suburban neighborhood was born with NPH. He was referred to as a "melon head." His head grew and grew. It became enormous, and scary to us children. Remembering him is sad. We children probably found him "funny-looking," because the unknown and grotesque can be funny, a limit to its frightening power. He was very smart, did very well at school, and didn't have a chance, because the shunt hadn't been perfected early enough for it to help him. He died at twenty, the normal life span of someone with NPH before the shunt.

Again, according to an NPH association: "700,000 people in the US have hydrocephalus, but only 20% are diagnosed." That's a hell of a lot of people diagnosed with other forms of dementia, all of them incurable.

The shunt operation was performed by a "highly regarded" neurosurgeon on February 12, 1996. I don't even recall his name, he was so little in the picture. He did the operation and disappeared from our lives. Later, I was told that surgeons were considered the "cowboys" of medicine, because you never saw them again, and they could—and can—be indifferent.

It was implanted, and Mother recuperated in the hospital. I vaguely remember visiting her in her room, her lying in bed, her head wrapped in white gauze, a hospital version of a turban. Immediately after the implantation of the shunt, Mother was more herself. She was released on February 26.

But at home, within days she began to have seizure activity, but the signs were not caught by the twenty-four-hour so-called skilled attendant we had hired through a useless, reassuring geriatric consultant.

Mother had uncontrollable bowel movements, a major symptom of seizure activity, but the attendant missed it.

Then she lost her bowels on the living room floor, which even the inexperienced or incompetent attendant couldn't miss. Mother had a grand mal seizure.

I raced over, and called an ambulance, and also contacted Dr. Z., the neurologist. In the ambulance, Mother, unconscious, was partially sitting up, and stitching an imaginary piece of fabric with an imaginary thread and needle. She had once been an extraordinary knitter and sewer, knitting coats and suits, not one stitch dropped.

We arrived in the ambulance at the hospital. Two men pushed Mother's gurney inside the large lobby.

No bed was free, I was told, though her neurologist, attached to this hospital, had called ahead and said a bed was promised. I said this repeatedly. It didn't matter.

I stood beside Mother in this large, austere lobby. She lay on the gurney stitching in the air. No bed available. After five minutes, the ambulance men said they had to leave for their next job. I stuttered No, or demanded No, and stared at my unconscious mother stitching in the air, stranded in the lobby. It was a uniquely awful and bizarre experience— Mother incapacitated, nowhere to go, and I was useless beside her. I must have been crying, stuck beside her, unable to do anything or think, and maybe the impatient or just hardworking ambulance men told me to speak again to the intake receptionist. I ran over and explained that a bed had been promised etc. Then I waited, standing there, feeling as close to hysterics as I've ever been. In the middle of the lobby, Mother lay stitching in the air.

A bed was found in the "new luxury wing," the receptionist said.

Mother and I, and I can't remember who else, probably the ambulance men, maybe a hospital staff person, were suddenly in the elevator going up to the new wing. A lot of this feels blank. I followed whomever, with Mother on the gurney.

The carpets were plush, I sank into them as I followed the gurney, leading to her plush private room. There was an atrium, lots of glass and potted plants in the halls, along the way. Her room looked like a new hotel's. I can't remember what pictures were on the walls, but the attempt had been made by the designers for it not to look like a hospital.

My New York sister arrived very soon. While she and I waited with Mother—the Carolina sister flew in and arrived that evening—we were served tea from a china teapot and matching cups, cream and sugar servers. Linen napkins. Maybe a vase with a flower. It was room service like a hotel's. The Carolina sister told me that, when she arrived, I was sitting on the floor, leaning against the wall in a hallway, weeping. I have no memory of that.

Quietly and in horror, we sisters observed Mother ceaselessly stitching the imaginary garment. Occasionally she was visited by a gaggle of interns who looked, conferred, shook their heads, walked away, did nothing. The nurses did nothing—I think we begged them for her meds. The interns came and went, two times, I believe it was. We were there waiting for about four hours.

The nasty neurologist finally arrived and saw her lying there stitching in the air, and was, I thought, alarmed. Then there was action, he made the call. He said nothing to us. It was as if we weren't there. I suppose he was embarrassed that his interns were so lame. Then Mother was whisked away to the Neurology ICU.

We were powerless and mystified by their inaction, and had earned many cups of brewed tea during our vigil. The care in the luxury wing of a major New York hospital proved to be incompetent and indifferent. It was no different from what it can be and often is for sick people in regular wards, say, without being served a complete tea service.

The nurses were changing shifts, we were told later—
the hospital's explanation for their neglect. The luxury ward.
Plush carpets. Good brewed tea. Lipstick on a pig.

The cowboy neurosurgeon had implanted a tube that was too
long. It bent or twisted, and stopped the fluid from passing
into her stomach. The fluid backed up and caused the shunt
to malfunction. The brain underwent significant seizure
activity.

In a procedure called a revision, the tube was shortened,
and Mother recovered enough to be sent home. Over ten
years, Mother would have six more revisions.

The shunt saves lives, but it malfunctions frequently: the
tube gets clogged just like ordinary plumbing. Each time
Mother's shunt malfunctioned, it had to be revised. After
the first revision, Mother wasn't progressing. We thought
Mother's shunt wasn't working, though the tube had been
shortened. Dr. Z. insisted it was fine, because he didn't
expect progress, given his prejudices, and he continued to
ridicule us. We went along, not with his judgment, always
questioning it, but felt beaten down by him. Maybe he could
tell it was working, somehow he knew the signs, and we
couldn't tell.

More wasted months, Mother's brain deteriorating, cells
dying. I'm not sure exactly how this occurred, but it was the

New York sister who broke free, liberated Mother from Dr. Z. She was determined to get Mother better and worked fiercely to help her. I believe she had heard about another neurosurgeon, Dr. R., and his work with the shunt. He operated primarily on children.

We consulted Dr. R., who was attached to a different hospital.

In his office, on January 31, 1997, and I remember that office also—clinical, not old-fashioned and comforting—we told Dr. R. we believed Mother's shunt wasn't working. His first question was: Has your mother had a shuntogram?

What?

A shuntogram.

A test exists?

Yes.

The next morning, February 1, 1997, Mother had a shuntogram. It wasn't a long test, it took maybe thirty minutes. I stood beside Mother while she was hooked up to it. It seemed a simple test, like the shunt itself, and it was not invasive. With immediate results.

The shunt was not working.

Dr. Z. had not even tried to find the truth. He must have known there was a shuntogram, how could he not, head of neurology at a big-deal hospital; but he didn't recommend it, because he thought—no, he knew he was right. We were emotional, and wrong. His opinion and prejudice were disastrous to Mother, to her brain's health—the longer the hydrocephalus built up, the more damage it did to her brain and functioning.

Then she needed another revision. She would need even more time to recover, and to what condition was unpredictable.

Dr. R. performed a revision, on February 14, 1997, and then, immediately, another was necessary, because blood had gotten into the tube, when her brain had bled. Mother underwent two surgeries, a second revision, within a week of each other. General anesthesia again. She was almost eighty-eight, physically strong, kind of amazing how she could arm wrestle even up to a month before she died. There was no choice but to do it, to give her any chance of a life, quality of life, again a rather benign concept about what is the difference between something and nothing.

After this revision or the next one in April, Mother didn't speak and could barely move for about eight months. She turned into dead weight. Two people needed to lift her just to get her to the bathroom. That's around when Lois was hired, and another woman to assist Lois with Mother.

The new neurosurgeon, Dr. R., candid and intelligent, was no cowboy, he was there. After Mother's shunt failed again, a year or so later, and another revision was needed, I asked, "Would you do this for your mother?" He considered it. Yes, I would, he said. And Mother had another revision. His belief was crucial.

My optometrist once explained that surgery is an art, not a science. A doctor's belief in a patient's possibilities is not an art or science, either. Optimism can't be taught, sadly; it can only be encouraged. Doctors present their views as pragmatic or realistic, when they may actually be dismissing cases as hopeless, like some do their geriatric patients. Most urgent to evaluate and notice: a doctor's expectations. They can determine your charge's ability to get better, get the right treatment. Some of my undergraduate writing students fault me for expecting too much of them. I tell them they're lucky I do, then I tell them this:

An experiment was performed by unsuspecting graduate psych students with rats. The students were divided into two groups, and given the same kind of rats to work with. But one group of students was told that their rats were incredibly smart, and the other was told their group were just ordinary rats, nothing special. Surprise!—the group who were told their rats were smart had trained their rats expecting good results. They had great results. The other group that had low or no expectations of success had underperforming "stupid" rats.

A doctor's expectations can help or hurt your charge.

Doctors may fear illness, may be phobic, and that could be why doctors become doctors. To ward off illness, to save not only others' lives but also their own. Because they had a sick mother or brother.

Some don't treat the elderly well enough, some are dismissive. The elderly represent mortality, and with their age greater fragility and a weaker immune system; the organs wear down, and there's more susceptibility to disease. Though doctors know aging and death are not diseases but natural events, the way birth and youth have been, and even with a big aging population, longer life spans, few doctors specialize in gerontology. Plastic surgery, gynecology and obstetrics, and dermatology are preferred.

It seemed implausible to believe Mother would ever emerge again as herself, or with much capacity. Over the years, she did progress. The brain repairs itself, finds and creates new pathways. And she was resilient and determined. If she had been younger when the NPH came on, she might have improved much, much more. If she had been shunted faster, she might have made much more progress.

We watched for signs of progress. Sometimes we watched so closely days were interrupted every few hours with phone calls, "She's doing better, she's doing worse." Her dependency forced conscious vigilance, and it was unconscious also. Days and nights dull and anxious, my life, like an oxymoron, was disturbed by emergencies, eruptions, and thudding repetitions.

Observing her undergoing this tortuous process—cognitive losses, surgery, procedures, slow recoveries—I dreaded the future, this ghost of time coming. I even felt, ridiculously, I was aging faster. My possibilities and fantasies were being stolen by Mother, whom I didn't love.

This composes a partial picture of the opening period. We sisters existed in an atmosphere of persistent worry. Foreboding was an unelected constituent of the everyday. Some days and weeks were better than others; then something would happen.

In the beginning, I imagined Mothercare would be similar to raising a child, one I had never wanted, being on call for another human being; but unlike a child she would not grow up and get stronger, more independent—she was failing, sometimes better, but still closing in on her death.

Before she became dependent, when she arrived in New York, Mother had opened a joint checking account with me. She had never before shown any faith in me as a responsible person, but I lived nearest to her. My New York sister was the executor of her will and her health proxy, but all three of us, her daughters, were involved in decisions about her health, her doctors, and caregivers.

The experience of hiring a caregiver, and a family's coordinating, cooperating, with a "live-in" companion, suggests material for a warped domestic novel. The home care attendants we employed were people of color. In this country, white writers could compose this story, and hopefully reckon honestly with prejudice, class and cultural differences, and possible or actual exploitation of undocumented workers. It would be a harsh tale, and hard to write, and I may be writing it.

When I could think clearly, when there wasn't an emergency, this was an ethical problem that wouldn't go away. Hiring a woman of color not born in the United States seemed a way to lessen complicity, a kind of elision, a veering away from the legacy of slavery. But it was only an angle. My privilege lived through the after-effects of colonialism and imperialism. The terms and effects were not abstract, they were personal, embodied in the women we were able to hire to care for Mother. I was conscious of it, but didn't forsake my privilege. I could have done that by living with Mother, changing my life for her. Even though I knew it was a way to resist that history, I couldn't, I couldn't live with her, just couldn't. I would have thrown myself out of one of the many windows in her apartment high up on the twenty-fourth floor.

Guilt was irrelevant, and self-serving.

Sometimes overwhelmed, I lost time and capacity to think clearly, if at all, about the ethical questions raised by her needs and our finances. Anxiety also produced quick decisions, and their unintended consequences rolled out. An outcome was a crapshoot, and you didn't even know you had rolled the dice.

What happened within twenty-four hours could fall together and apart simultaneously. Expectations of a normal day, of an ordinary day, lost cogency.

At first, and generally, the companion will be seen as a helper for the patient and family, especially in the initial months of her employment. The family doesn't know the helper, and she doesn't know them. A family adjusts or does not to her, and she does or does not to them.

From her point of view, she is an employee of a patient and a family, who are kind or mean, relaxed, tense, generous, cheap. She becomes part of the family, ineluctably, though she is never, really, because she can be fired. One can't fire family. Whatever the family is, whatever problems it has, will exert a unique pressure on her. She has to manage not just her patient but also the patient's family.

This is its own kind of relationship, unlike any other, and unlike any I have ever known. If I were to write a novel whose protagonist was a companion, she would be mysterious, intelligent, charming, enigmatic, a good worker with ambition and ambivalence.

Early in Mother's days of incapacity, a number of women lived with her, and I remember some distinctly. Lois stands out—efficient, driven, energetic. She seemed unbelievably great when she was with Mother. Lois spent the day with Mother, she didn't live with her, and motivated Mother, made her get up from bed, her chair, made her walk and do exercises. But after four months, Lois moved to Florida, and recommended her cousin, Sharon, who turned out to be trouble or just a bad fit. Maybe she was troubled. I liked Sharon well enough, but didn't get to know her, and she wasn't with Mother long. When she was fired, euphemistically let go, I was away at the MacDowell Colony, writing, and I didn't know what the problems were, out of the loop, but Mother had complained about Sharon mostly to my New York sister.

Later, and for months, Sharon phoned me, perplexed, upset, she didn't think she was a problem, she wanted me to explain why she was let go. I couldn't say: Mother didn't like you. But they had argued a lot. Arguing with a patient, especially one with brain damage or dementia, is futile and a problem in itself. Sharon called me for a few years, especially on Mother's birthday, and asked, "How's Mother doing?" I felt terrible, again with a unique problem. I tried to comfort her, who had liked Mother, and was very sad, even mystified, about being fired, but I couldn't explain it to her, give her a good reason that wouldn't hurt her feelings.

Lois refused to speak to us again. We had fired her cousin. I once phoned Lois, who answered but then pretended not to be herself. When I said, "I know it's you," she told me I was confusing her with her cousin. I rarely confuse voices, and it was absurd. She was adamant I had it wrong, she wasn't Lois. She was furious. Again, an extraordinary situation, her fury unexpected, and this experience, of a woman pretending not to be herself, strange and disturbing. We had liked Lois so much, she had been wonderful with Mother, and now she hated us. We hadn't considered how firing Sharon would affect her. Maybe we could have told her our concerns. But even if we had, the same decision would have been taken. Would our telling her have quelled her anger, should we have consulted her.

I keep returning to and reflecting on the word "firing," as in, to fire an employee. I imagine its origins, and think a common usage of "fire" might be related to throwing someone or something into a fire, to get rid of them, or it. Burning people alive. "To burn" is colloquial now, different but related. Maybe Foucault mentioned these etymologies in *Discipline and Punish*. I'll check.

Awful, regrettable, weird incidents and events accumulated, too many to recall. Some, many probably, are repressed. The bad times presented new kinds of stress, and too much happened too fast to recall most of it in detail.

Another live-in companion wore great hats. I thought of her as Hats but her name was Doris. When Hats stayed with Mother, who was barely moving or eating, after her first surgeries and revisions, masses of food disappeared. I shopped every week and bought cold cuts, bread, cookies, cheese, meat, fish, fruit. Way too much food, but I didn't know what I was doing. The food was always gone. Our phone bill ballooned. In the 1990s, calling a Brooklyn or Queens number—718—from Manhattan cost. I paid the bills and gave Hats a pass. I just wanted someone there to relieve us, me.

Doris was beautiful, a big woman and hefty. I thought she must eat a lot to maintain her weight. Also I figured it was boring to care for a semi-comatose patient, so she probably ate a lot of the time. But all of this seemed unimportant compared with having her attend to Mother, to be there and siphon off the steady drain of Mother, and cater to Mother's requirements.

Hats was, I'm pretty sure, a U.S. citizen. A few women

who cared for Mother were, but not all of them, and most important, the woman who was her companion for ten years was not.

Over those years, I visited her or was on call almost every day, then every few days. Mother hovered over me and my sisters like a stationary drone. It became after a while, five years maybe, my irregular regular life.

I didn't want to be there, at Mother's. My New York sister was much less reluctant, and I believe my reluctance strained our relationship some or disappointed her in me— relationships strain under this kind of persistent stress, this particular tension among siblings and their sense of duty. All of this digs deep into a family's craters, its collective psyche, if there is such a thing.

There's no easy time for any family or group of close friends around sickness. When a parent is terminally ill, the weight has a particularity, a special gravity. You will lose a parent, you have just two, usually, though families today might have several. Still, that parent figure in your life is unique. And a family is a complex, its own kind of complex formed of many elements. It presents with preexisting psychological conditions.

As children, we were the Tillman Sisters, the Three Musketeers, united against "the parents," all for one, one for all. "All" were my two older sisters, way ahead of me in age and understanding, the birth-position leaders. I fell in line, wanting always to be a part of them. "All for one" was and is powerful, though as I grew up I recognized how different we were from one another.

We had differences about Mother: how she should be "handled," cared for, down to which vacuum cleaner she should have. Our disagreements might not have been resolved perfectly but adequately, so we could go on. A decided practicality among us encouraged getting along, figuring it out. We were goal-oriented. Our feelings and history with Mother were not the same, our ideas for her care were not, also, but we worked together for her sake.

I don't speak for my sisters' feelings and thoughts, only mine. I believe we very consciously worked around our emotions, attachments, and detachments. I think all of us were conscious of the possibility of estrangement and didn't want it to come to that, ever. I don't remember ever discussing this with my sisters, it was implicit and unspoken. Some families break, divide, and form divisions that last until death. We didn't want to abandon each other—or Mother, though I sometimes wished I could.

It wasn't easy for any of us. I had sleepless nights, I bet they did also.

✦

My schedule was my own, as they say. I wasn't required to show up at a job or in an office until I was teaching. That happened when I took a position at the University at Albany, in the English Department. I taught in the spring, starting in 2002, and then my ability to be on call was limited. Otherwise, I was ready to run or cab it to her apartment anytime.

My life felt narrower, and not my own. I gave up some of my life, that's the kind of thought I had, common to us who don't want to do what we feel obliged to do. A sacrifice. I rebelled against that loss of freedom, especially in the first few years. Adjusting was hard, then I did, but never completely, especially when it was my turn to do a weekend at Mother's apartment, then hours felt like years. Prosaically, I was dying on a vine, imprisoned. Immature or silly or useless feelings, and nothing to do about any of it.

From the age of six, I had disliked my mother, but I didn't wish her dead. I gave her caregivers as wide a berth as I could. I wanted them to care for her, I wanted to trust them. I didn't know any better than to trust them, and in some ways I didn't know anything, and was selfish also. I wanted Mother to be handled by others, chores and things be done by others. Handling this novel situation stymied me—the relationship between caregiver and Mother, how to create an equitable situation among us sisters. None of us knew the best way, we tried to find ways, we improvised, tried our best. I thought I knew my limits, I thought I should have limits, but limits and boundaries are erased and erected and erased again. There is nothing stable when dealing with a parent or friend whose condition is essentially unstable. Still, I looked for that, a steady state.

Until we the family knew better, Hats filled Mother's pillboxes. But she mistakenly doubled Mother's antiseizure medication, Depakote. Mother slowed down even more, to a halt. We figured it out, then my New York sister and I filled the boxes ever after. We kept close track, and her future longtime caregiver did, also. Mother's meds and dosages changed with her condition and her needs. We kept lists, and kept modifying them.

This pill list is for 2005 (Depakote 250 mg added at the end of July 2005, against seizures).

Breakfast:
Reminyl, 8 mg
Diamox, 125 mg
Lexapro, 5 mg
Lanoxin, 0.125 mg
Naproxen, 375 mg (she had been taking that for a long time because of terrible migraines; Dr. A. wondered if naproxen

might have forestalled the onset of her NPH; I wondered if
the migraines were an early warning)

Norvasc, 5 mg

Namenda, 10 mg

Tanganil, 500 mg (OTC, against dizziness, available only in
France; my friend Sidonie mailed the boxes from Paris)

Loratadine (generic Claritin)—every other day 10 mg. This
alternates with Benadryl, which is taken at night

Multivitamin, one pill

Rhinocort nasal spray, one puff each nostril

Premarin cream—use Q-tip to apply to inside of nostrils

Locoid cream—outside of nostrils

Mylanta—3/4 tablespoon, 1 spoon if necessary

Optivar liquid—one drop each eye if itchy

Lunchtime:

Same dosages of Namenda, Diamox, and Tanganil;
plus omega-3; vitamin C; *Cordyceps*, 700 mg

Bedtime:

Glucosamine, 1 pill

Calcium, 1 pill, 1000 mg

Benadryl—every other night, alternates with loratadine

Rhinocort, one puff each nostril

Clenia cream—outside of nostrils

Bacitracin—outside of nostrils

Mylanta, 3/4 tablespoon, 1 spoon if necessary

Optivar liquid, one drop each eye if itchy

Xalatan, one drop each eye (keep refrigerated)

Premarin cream—rarely, and only for nosebleeds—inside of nostrils

In 1987, when she lived alone in Florida, after my father died, Mother's mitral valve was replaced with a pig's. Normally, a pig's valve lasts about ten years; but Mother's lasted until she died, for twenty years. Her internist, Dr. A., said he realized, because Mother had become so inactive, her valve lasted much longer. That was propitious, because Mother told me she regretted having had the operation, its aftermath was too painful, and for about a year or two, she kept saying she wished she hadn't had it. This was surprising. Mother understood the risks of not having it, becoming incapacitated, dying sooner. Maybe then, still in Florida, which she hated, she wanted to die. Or at least not be alive. She was kept on a heart med, digoxin. Also, her nose became very sensitive, because of postnasal drip. She had sores inside it. Her nose ran and ran and also caused irritations outside the nostrils, which accounts for all the nostril medications.

Dr. A. became Mother's point man, her medical administrator, in touch and collaborating with her other doctors, so her meds would not work at cross-purposes and cause other problems, which often happens. Elderly patients probably suffer more from being overmedicated than undermedicated, and can get sicker.

After Hats was let go, and I don't remember how—I once courted her favor, buying a delicious French cake for her birthday and giving her a gift of two hundred dollars—I realized that, inside her voluminous weekend bag, she carried home food every weekend. We hired other companions for those weekends, though my New York sister often stayed with Mother, much more than I did. Sometimes I felt guilty, mostly I rationalized and tried to forget.

Hats had been paid a minimum wage, and the food she carried home helped her financially. It wasn't right, I told myself, taking the food, but it was nothing in the greater reality—Mother's care, first, and the economic and social inequities. I couldn't stand on principle when some principles were being stretched from our side. Nothing was right about this situation.

A few more poor hires, bad fits. One was Patsy, a small, pretty woman from the Philippines who seemed to love Mother to death. When I took Mother for her monthly appointment with Dr. Z., the arrogant neurologist, Patsy and Mother slumped on the couch in his waiting room. They

rolled around and giggled like five-year-olds. I had no idea
what to make of it or what to do; I did nothing.

Patsy slept in Mother's bed at night to comfort her, which
seemed kind and Mother liked it, but she proved to be a lu-
natic, and we had to fire her. This was accomplished—her
firing—through an eldercare consultant my New York sister
had hired, smooth and reassuring, utterly ineffective. But
Patsy's firing was upsetting, anyway. Firing people is always
terrible. Patsy was nice but a little mad, crazy. She was hired
through the eldercare consultant who also had us hire the
woman who didn't recognize Mother's grand mal seizure,
after her first bad surgery. The woman was supposed to have
special knowledge of Mother's situation, supposed to know
what could happen. She didn't see the signs of a grand mal
seizure.

This consultant, whose company had a fancy, impressive name, was supposed to keep in touch with Mother's doctors, help us find people. We were, in the beginning, at a loss and very vulnerable, and she made us feel we would be relieved of so many problems. Untrue, and ironically, her people were problems—and she was incredibly expensive. The attendants she chose for Mother were incompetent or nuts, and paying her a fortune was ridiculous. I remember one bill for one month being about $1,600. She had listed everything, a detailed list of nothing. None of it added up to her fee. She was fired.

Over the eleven years, emergencies, domestic conflicts, had me racing to Mother's apartment. One morning, I stood beside her and watched bright red blood gush from her mouth. I don't know how but I took her to the ER, by cab or ambulance, I can't recall. I knew what the problem was: she had become nauseated taking Tylenol with codeine. I do too. And couldn't stop throwing up. After vomiting violently, her esophagus tore. I didn't know that, but Dr. A. did.

Mother spent all day in the hospital, undergoing unnecessary tests. I told the intern in charge, Mother lying on a bed in the ER, codeine was the problem. We both vomited from it. He ignored me and ordered unnecessary tests, even though in an encyclopedia of illnesses, a handbook right beside him on a table, the first side effect associated with codeine was vomiting.

Mother was wheeled off for tests, somewhere, and, hours later, no one could find her. She had been lost in a hospital hallway. I raced through the halls and found her lying, impassively, out of it and on a lonely gurney.

Interminable, enervating waiting—hospitals suck life from you. This visit or another, a social worker asked my New York sister and me to come to her office, where she asked questions that puzzled my sister. The social worker was assessing us, to see if we were abusing Mother. It happens, the elderly are abused. Anyone can be abused, wealthy or poor, when incapacitated, everyone is prey to sadists. Being suspected of that, definitely unpleasant.

In a hospital, your sick parent in a room, she's in pain, moaning, crying, or something weird is happening, you run to the nurse's station looking for immediate help. Maybe no one pays attention. Then you shout for help. It happens. Watching someone in pain breaks every rule of decorum. In that plush hospital room, waiting and waiting for a doctor to see Mother, who needed immediate care, worry mounting, I was reminded of that scene in *Terms of Endearment* when Shirley MacLaine, playing the mother, witnesses her dying daughter, played by Debra Winger, suffering, in agony. MacLaine totally loses it, runs to the nurses' station, rages and screams at the nurses to help her daughter. She

doesn't stop until one of them goes to help her. MacLaine
calms down, stands up straighter, arranges her blouse, pats
herself down, literally, to straighten herself out, pull herself
together. These gestures were perfect visual metaphors.

I will say, without caution, when a parent becomes dependent, a family is inundated with surprising, bewildering, and
constant, complicated issues. Never-before-faced issues. It
will be shocked by the magnitude and mystery and consequence of this new and old fact of life. Unforeseeable and
nasty accidents and diagnoses present themselves, and families may do research or react impulsively, they may deliberate
or become numb with trepidation. Often families are evis-
cerated by their differences. Often only one child cares for
the parent, and all burdens rest on them. But when several
adults are in charge, a hell of resentments and conflicts can
overwhelm functioning.

The unspoken and unconscious emerge from historical
and psychological relationships with parents and siblings.
All of this history affects individual attitudes and choices,
which can vitiate and deflate everyone involved. Charged
feelings lurk in interpretations and decisions, the terrain is
treacherous, and bombs from previous wars detonate under the intensity of deeply felt emotions. A family or group
of friends will work together for the greater good of the

patient, or it will fall apart from divisiveness. Many do. We sisters, her daughters, held together, our goal to keep Mother alive and as well as could be expected, for as long as possible.

One woman lived with Mother for close to ten years.

Nothing about this situation is simple, a person doesn't take care of another person twenty-four hours a day, for years, without involvement in ways I, for one, had never encountered or expected. Hiring another person to be in charge of a parent's daily life, her body, her meals, pricks an adult child's conscience and unconscious. I was unprepared and didn't know what was right, wrong. Ethical issues arose about situations I had never thought would occur. That's a young human being's right, it's said, to live in the moment. I was aware of death and dying from the age of five, but wasn't thinking about illness, not chronic illness. My family was physically healthy, fortunately, good genes, no fried food. Psychological issues, that's another thing. I thought the psychiatrist treating my uncle Al was a family doctor, like our Dr. Robbins in Woodmere.

Sometimes passages from Virginia Woolf's diary came to mind, her anguish over her servants, their feelings, children, husbands, cooking, competence, their mistakes, salary—justice, generally. A caregiver is not a nineteenth-century

servant but a service provider. Still, Mother's life entwined
with her companion's, and the other way around. Mother
depended upon her; and the more she did, the happier I was,
the more time off—freedom—I had. I could be at home and
write, or escape. Walking away from Mother's apartment, I
breathed air that wasn't hers. That felt free. This might sound
strange. Maybe not.

An employee who lives inside the walls of her employer
suffers and benefits from the habits of a family in ways no
other worker does. There is a feudal aspect to the relationship, tenant and landowner, an overriding psychological
aspect to "living together." Our last and longest-running
caregiver was terrific with Mother, active with her, took
her to the theater, movies, museums, would go out with
her every day, to appointments for manicures, pedicures,
haircuts. She would accompany Mother to her doctors' appointments, checkups, and all of her doctors trusted her to
report accurately to us, her daughters, about her condition,
and what new meds she needed if any. She was trusted. We
trusted her.

Frances was of Indian descent from a Caribbean island.
She was a country girl. New York City scared Frances, then
she embraced it like a new friend. At first, her salary was
rock-bottom, because we hired her from an agency that
placed undocumented workers. I didn't think about it much
at first, desperate for help, I didn't put it to myself like

that—undocumented. I avoided thinking about it. Frances was naive, untrained, and we were her first employers. Or her second, if counting her first client, a comatose man who died almost immediately in her care but not because of it.

We were really her first clients. Frances didn't know the rules of the game of her job; she was a novice skilled only in caring for her own children. I didn't know the rules, either, or if there were rules a family had to follow. We all seemed to be making it up as we went along with Frances's needs and disposition.

She had left her children and husband to come to the United States to earn money to send home. This is typical in our unjust world. Her room, food, phone, electric, Internet were included in her weekly salary. The Carolina sister bought her a computer. There were other perks through the years, including money for her son to attend a vocational school here. Her salary was raised often, but it was never more than $640 a week. She had a paid week off, then two paid weeks off, weekends off, Christmas week off, New Year's off, Thanksgiving week off, though it wasn't a meaningful holiday to her. The New York sister stayed with Mother on weekends much more than I did, so I usually took over when Frances had her vacations and days off. Her weeks off were a misery to me.

✦

During the first years especially, Mother hallucinated, her dreams real to her; in one, a suitcase was lost, where was it? and she insisted on this sometimes for days. Where was it, it was lost. What had we done with it? She became more and more agitated, and if I said, There's no lost suitcase, she'd become furious. Sometimes she cried. It's typical behavior for people who have memory loss. I came to think the suitcase was holding her past, its loss represented her lost past. Or the suitcase contained her lost memories.

Sometimes Mother would see a man in her room and become frightened. It was pointless to tell her it was a dream, pointless to refute her. Irrationality proves rationality dumb, telling Mother no man had been there was in fact silly. Being rational is dumb when challenging the irrational—nothing convinces. It's especially unreasonable to attempt to enforce rationality on someone who has lost some of her power to reason. Mother's repetitious questions were maddening. Where was her handbag, her necklace. The suitcase. The saddest question was about her husband, my father, Nathan Tillman.

In the first years, she didn't remember he was dead. She believed he'd abandoned her, just left her. Where was he? she'd ask. Where's Nat? Where's Daddy? He had been dead since 1984. When, finally, I'd tell her, "He's dead," she'd cry out, her shock real. She would say, "Why didn't you tell me? I didn't know about his funeral. Was I at his funeral?" Each time she learned he was dead, she reacted the same way until her brain had recovered more memory, and she knew he was dead, he was never coming back. She never stopped missing him, the love of her life.

One morning at breakfast, she said, seemingly out of nowhere, "I miss sex." In all my life with her, she had never said anything about sex or even allowed for the existence of it. Never, except that she once said she would kill me if I wasn't a virgin when I married. Laughable but awful.

Mother had a capacity for reason sometimes, but was unreasonable the next hour, and it was confusing. She could be coherent, in her right mind, then erratic, sometimes here, there, nowhere. I had to learn—we all did—not to force her to make sense, it was useless. Her frustration rose, mine did, and sense didn't emerge. I learned to say yes, listen, nod, comfort her, and hope she'd forget in a while and go on to other things. She confused names, hardly a problem. She called my David "Jimmy." When she was lucid, I asked her, Why do you call him Jimmy? She laughed and said, "I don't know."

The New York sister had a car, and would drive Mother to restaurants or go on shopping trips with her. Mother loved going out with her, loved being driven around the city, taken to excellent restaurants. She loved getting out of the house. Of course.

When the Joyce Theater, which features contemporary dance, presented its new season, the New York sister bought season tickets for her and Mother. She drove
Mother and stopped right in front of the theater on Eighth
Avenue, and someone from the Joyce would come outside
and help Mother to her seat, while my sister found a park-
ing spot, never easy in Manhattan. We thanked the theater
for their kindness, and sent a letter they pinned to their
office wall.

Sometimes it was Frances who accompanied Mother to
the Joyce, often she took her to plays, mostly matinees, and
movies. As Mother's hearing grew worse, dances, concerts,
and musical theater worked better than straight plays. Frances did so much with Mother, and activity was urgent. She
might otherwise atrophy sitting on her comfortable chair in
front of the TV or reading a book. The elderly need exercise;
their lives depend upon it, in fact.

For some years Frances and she were members of the
YMCA on West Twenty-third Street, and took classes together. A young man taught the exercise class, and Mother,
who liked men, especially handsome ones, would light up
at the sight of him. When Mother was no longer capable of
traveling to the Y, he was paid to give her sessions at home.
Sometimes I was there, and watched. Lifting and swing-
ing her arms took more effort than I would have imagined,
but Mother strove to do it. She wanted to succeed, and she

wanted his approval. Mother had been athletic when she was young, and was a strong walker into her late eighties. She had strength and resilience. Still, it took a lot of effort, and I saw firsthand how a body diminishes.

I had given up tennis, stopped running, all of that, so I'd like to say this was a wake-up call, but I didn't exactly wake up. I was made conscious of the ill effects of inactivity, which I partly ignored. I walked a lot, and told myself that was good enough.

But I had once asked a doctor what's best to do as you get older. He said, "Stretch." I didn't then, but now I do. Stephen Jay Gould, the biologist, when asked his advice, said, "Get a flu shot every year." I do. Mother's internist gave Frances flu shots, and would see her as a patient or advise or prescribe a drug if needed. She was a healthy woman, though quite overweight; in time her diet became better.

Most of the caregivers we employed briefly, before Frances arrived, were barely active with Mother, and not enthusiastic about taking her outside, going places with her. Frances might have been wary, at first, of this very big city; she might have been anxious moving around in a big city, but she didn't cater to her fears. She accompanied Mother everywhere Mother wanted to go. Frances took Mother for haircuts, to have her nails done; they went to neighborhood parks, where Mother watched the birds and in the spring and summer looked at flowers. I believed Frances enjoyed these outings, though she didn't tell me that. But she never complained, either. She did her job well.

About a year after Frances started living with Mother, she discovered her husband had taken up with another woman. Devastated, her faith tested—she was a religious Catholic—she was deeply hurt. Her husband's betrayal undid her in ways I didn't know, and way more than I apprehended. Her anger rose, often misplaced and unfocused. In some sense, I think she blamed us. If she weren't working for Mother, and here to help her children, give them a better life, she and her husband having decided that together, he wouldn't have strayed. If she hadn't been forced into this situation because of economic inequities, she would still have her husband. That could have been true. And we could afford to hire her, making us part of this awful end, and benefiting from that system.

After Mother's many revisions, so much scar tissue had formed in her stomach that the tube couldn't discharge there, and again it had stopped working, Dr. A. told us it would have to be threaded through her jugular vein into her heart. If an infection developed, he explained to her and us, she would get an infection in her heart and die.

Mother was practical, tough-minded, calm about medical issues, her own also. When I was a child and had double-lobar pneumonia, running a high fever, our family doctor allowed me to stay home because he trusted that she would be a good nurse. About sickness, Mother was very good, and also good at diagnosis. She could notice something on your skin, say, and tell you what it was. Or tell you to have it checked.

Mother agreed to have that last revision, a tube laced under her skin through her jugular vein to her heart, and chance death rather than live without life. When she was lucid, Mother faced hard decisions dead on. Sensible, I thought, to die rather than vegetate.

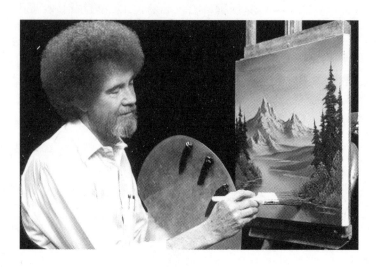

Bob Ross

Mother started painting when I was an adolescent, attending a weekly art class at the Community House, located in Inwood. My older sisters were no longer living at home, for the most part, they were in college or working in the city. She had more time for herself. After school, I was often alone with her.

Inwood was the "poor" town of the so-called Five Towns. Mostly African Americans and Italian Americans lived there, lower- and lower-middle-class people—the maids, handymen, and gardeners where I grew up. Strict divisions— race, religion, class—were enforced by neighborhood and school, which I didn't become aware of until I was ten, and away for two weeks at Girl Scout camp—I don't know why, but I wanted merit badges. (I recently learned that Sylvia Plath was a serious Girl Scout and wanted badges, too.) It was a different population from my hometown, I was the only Jewish girl in a group of fifty-four, and there were only white people. Then I started to recognize class and race seg- regation. Life at home shifted, I saw it differently, because of these distinctions.

Mother's going to the Community House, in Inwood, for art classes, socializing with its social workers and cli- ents, meant she crossed visible and invisible lines. One of her close friends there, Fred, was African American and a social worker. I remember he was a genial man, and had a limp.

She was an amateur painter, with untutored talent. Her first paintings were copies of famous-artist paintings—Van Gogh's of worker's shoes. Her paintings were representa- tional, realistic—an orange cat; a portrait of me looking like a romantic heroine; a copy of a Manet, I forget which one. But she had stopped painting after my father died. He complimented her paintings excessively.

Then her condition struck.

When she was better, the shunt working, she was able, capable, and started painting again. Now her paintings were abstract. She would say, "I'm going to paint a cat," but it wasn't close to a cat, anything but a cat. It was an eye, inside a mass of white, a cloud of white. It was what her mind was seeing. Or what her brain was seeing. The change was fascinating, worthy of study, and I took photographs. I showed them to Dr. A. Her determination to paint and knit, to relearn, was admirable. Her resilience was admirable. And encouraging. She was unusual in this way, because she helped herself.

About the third year Frances lived with Mother, things went missing. My New York sister noticed a sweater or two, a piece of costume jewelry, nothing precious, were gone. Maybe Frances's friends were taking things or something was just misplaced. Many friends visited her when she first began living with Mother. Small things disappeared. It didn't bother me, because nothing mattered compared with the much tougher problems of caring for Mother. And, besides, Frances was consistently good with her, and Mother

didn't complain about Frances the way she had about the
other women who watched over her.

Knives and forks would disappear. I didn't bring it up.
One night Frances told me, "I throw silverware away." She
said it forthrightly as if it were just one of her eccentricities.
Frances spoke with no affect and didn't look at me; she was
at the sink. She said she would throw knives, spoons, and
forks into the garbage can. It was just a thing she did. But
the silverware had to be replaced, and it cost money to do
that. She didn't trouble to say, I'll try not to do that again.
I should have pushed it, maybe, to understand what was
going on, why she was doing this nonsensical thing. But I
accepted it as her odd behavior, everyone is a little nuts, and
I trusted her.

Her friends would have lunch together in Mother's dining room alcove. They'd sleep over and shower there. Her
children lived in her room with her for a week or two. We
paid for her oldest daughter's wedding party. We did what
we could within our limits. Frances's oldest daughter was
married in the Catholic church on the next block. She had
become very involved in her church, whose choir conductor
and his wife were her new friends. Eventually, they brought
their baby girl to visit her and Mother. Mother adored the
little girl, who, at two years old, was very tall, and appeared
to be five. She would run to Mother as soon as she entered
the apartment. Mother loved her avid attention.

✦

In the early years, we daughters worked to discover how best to help her. Mother was considered an unusual medical case. Maybe there was new research for old problems.

One depressing misadventure: I took Mother for evaluation by a research group on aging and dementia, affiliated with her hospital. Their rooms were situated in a dismal basement, a project noticeably underfunded, the way aging itself was then, and could be still, and noticeably understudied.

They tested and videotaped her. Mother wasn't a perfect NPH candidate because her gait was never an NPH gait. She did well, in their terms, on some tests and badly on others. During all her visits, her responses did not consistently fit their parameters for NPH.

The researchers were unenthusiastic, dull men, who viewed Mother as an object of study. Brain damage had made her remarkably compliant—she was not belligerent the way she mostly had been—and seeing her attempt to do what they asked of her—walk a straight line, remember these words—was heartrending, even pathetic, especially since she mattered to them only as she confirmed or disconfirmed their theories. They didn't believe she had NPH.

When Mother walked better, attended the theater with her caregiver, or took the bus to Bloomingdale's to buy a suit— pale pink—for her upcoming birthday party, made jokes, was painting or reading, when she recovered capacity in ways that were medically unexpected, I imagined returning with her to those dull researchers. She would show them they had no idea what they had seen, they had no idea how to test anyone.

It remained a fantasy, just as suing Dr. Z., the arrogant neurologist, did.

Some days I wanted to take everyone to court, a godless Job-poor-me, why did this have to happen, a put-upon-by-life feeling. Yeah, poor me, poor everyone.

"I never saw a wild thing // sorry for itself. // A small bird will drop frozen dead from a bough // without ever having felt sorry for itself."

—D. H. LAWRENCE

"Life, I fancy, would very often be insupportable, but for the luxury of self-compassion."

—GEORGE GISSING

The brain grows new cells. The way the shunt drained fluid, more or less, from one hour to the next, affected her physically and mentally. Some days she was remarkably lucid, some days she wasn't. Some days she walked better. We figured it had to do with the flow of CSF. She did have some permanent brain damage from the pressure before the shunt was implanted, and from when it wasn't working. If it wasn't working, all her symptoms returned, and if not redone, she would go back to zero.

Dr. Z., the arrogant neurologist, who is dead, laughed at our concerns and told us the shunt was working when it wasn't. It may have been right to sue him for malpractice, but I thought then, and told my New York sister, it would absorb more of our time, our flagging spirits and energy, and crush us more than we were. Maybe I was wrong. Maybe we should have. But he's dead.

Mother had an appointment with her new neurologist, Dr. D., affiliated with the neurosurgeon's hospital, and, initially, he seemed dubious Mother could make progress. At first he struck me as dour, even grim, not particularly engaged with her.

During a second or third visit, Mother was completely inattentive, not talking, not at all lucid. This was during that very bad stretch after her third revision. The Carolina sister was right beside me, across from Dr. D. By now she spent one weekend every six to eight weeks with Mother.

I asked, "Isn't there anything you can do. Anything. Can't you try something?"

Mother's eight months of immobility—a kind of semi-comatose state—were desperate days. "Can't you give her something to help her brain?" Dr. D. thought, his forehead actually wrinkled. "Maybe Ritalin," he said. "It can activate aging brains."

After taking Ritalin for two weeks, Mother spoke again. When we brought her back to him, she was so changed, he was startled. Seeing her renewed liveliness and humor, he became playful with her, and she responded. Mother liked men.

Helpers are critically important in getting the best out of doctors, aides, hospitals. It's critical to be bold—your charges can't defend or help themselves. Critical to do your own research, to encourage doctors to explore and try other and different techniques, tactics, ideas. The elderly especially are seen as dead weight to the medical industry. Not all doctors dismiss them, but some do. Their cases can be depressing. Many don't get better. Some can improve and lead better lives.

I guarded time for my writing, getting to it whenever I could, and felt defeated when time was hijacked. It was all too human, unforgivable and forgivable. Since I wrote at home, I was the daughter available to pick up a package of adult diapers and shampoo or a prescription, then walk over. Luckily, my sisters understood my need to get away, spend a month or more at MacDowell, an artists' and writers' retreat. I was a resident, or fellow, many times, grateful beyond words for the luxury of writing without interruption. I stayed in contact with my sisters and Mother's companion, not daily, probably every other day. I wasn't there, physically, which was freedom. And I dreaded any call, the one that would make me leave.

I spoke by phone with my psychoanalyst, Dr. G., once a week, lying on the floor of an office where I could make private calls. He came into my life not long after Mother became sick. The pressures around her care, her daily needs, the erratic days and nights, and the differences among us sisters about her care, about how we felt about her, made me crazy. I couldn't sleep.

Mother's destiny was oppressive but finite, I reminded myself, but every day held the drone of discussions about her health, moods, new and old aides. The weirdest thing: I never entirely became used to it. I just coped better. The sameness and differences, the expected is unexpected, the unexpected expected, it is always out of sync with what you once called your life.

People who do this work professionally have shorter life spans. The work, the necessary patience, the long hours exhaust a person. Time goes slowly, seems to stall, to suspend. And time is what human beings have or don't.

We sisters all had to give time to Mother, change the way we lived; we New York sisters were local, and called upon more. Generally I showed sympathy to Mother, but it came at a cost other than time, my emotional health, because Mother's plight burdened me, burdened us all.

An irony not lost on me was how uncaring she was. Close friends said I didn't talk about how I felt, I didn't complain. I became a stalwart soldier, and miserable. No consolation came from discussing Mothercare problems, and sympathy didn't help me, it actually made me feel sorrier for myself.

There were so many issues, but nothing could be changed, her condition would get better or not, take time, she would die sooner or later, her future was unpredictable. Everyone's future is, but we family hung on our mother's. How long would this go on.

I could have done or behaved differently, maybe.

Put her in a home. My therapist kept saying we should do that.

I succumbed to innate pressures and external ones, to be a good daughter, a good sister. Some days I felt fine; some days I despaired of my superactive superego.

My husband, David, is a musician; he plays bass and/or tuba in many bands. One midday he was gigging with the Metropolitan Klezmer band outdoors, in Abe Lebewohl Park in front of St. Mark's Church. I think it was a fine day in May. This was before Mother was sick, and she attended the concert. When the set was over, she walked up to David and said, "Your instrument doesn't play the melody." She also told him she didn't like klezmer music.

Mother was blunt, worse, she was insensitive consistently.

Her consistency—it's important that children have that in a parent—enabled me not to become more neurotic than I am.

David played with the singer-songwriter Nora York's band for years, so Nora, who also taught singing, agreed to give Mother private lessons. Because of her longtime musical relationship with David, he was her very trusted bass player.

Mother had always fancied herself an opera singer. She had several illusions about herself, including that she was perfect. Christ, she told me, wasn't, because he was "too perfect." Her logic didn't fail when it served her. It was hard sometimes not to be jealous of her unflappable narcissism.

Learning how to breathe correctly to sing correctly helped Mother's balance and walking. It was an unexpected, positive consequence of the singing lessons. Breathing affects balance, of course.

After one of her gigs, Nora said to me, solemnly, that she understood me better after working with my mother. She didn't say why, but looked at me with compassion. I understood that she had witnessed Mother's meanness and selfishness. I didn't know the whole story until much later.

Mother had many helpers including a Swedish massage therapist, who actually was Swedish, and also a lesbian, and called herself a lesbian, this was around 2000. She worked on Mother once a week. Mother had some arthritis in her lower back. When Mother found out the massage therapist was a lesbian, she became upset. That's a terrible prejudice, I told her, not to like a person because they're Black or Jewish or gay. Mother understood, got it fast, and her attitude changed instantly. Kind of incredible, actually.

Visiting her apartment, I'd hear them roaring with laughter through her closed bedroom door. Mother came to adore her massage therapist. One afternoon, Mother told me they were going to get married, they were lesbians.

Mother was a strange creature, intolerant, angry, sometimes but rarely open, able to learn. She was far from a "good listener." She was smart, her neuroses never acknowledged by her, her character misshapen by episodes early in her life, ones I had no knowledge of. She said of her mother, as she said of herself: She was perfect. It seemed obvious neither one could be. The only anecdote I know about her mother, my grandmother—whom I don't remember, or I do, only because of a scene in an 8 mm film—comes from a story Mother wrote, and never finished, about adopting our cat, the astonishing Griselda.

"There was always a cat or kitten in my background. My mother said a cat was a necessity or the house would be overrun with rats and mice and even vermin. You see we were living (some would say existing) on the East Side in the heart of squalor and home could never be home unless it harbored a cat. I always suspected that in my mother's case the cat was not, as she reiterated time and again, housed as a necessity but rather because of her love for the feline species. I recall the solemnity in our home because of my mother's sadness whenever some misfortune or accident would befall the cat of the moment . . ."

She never talked about her father, except to say he had a small wooden box, like a jewelry box, where he kept his treasures. No one was allowed to see the box's contents, and Mother hated him for that, though she never said that. He was selfish, secretive. She was also very jealous of her older sister. Mother's mother favored her first child and daughter, who had blond hair and blue eyes, who was sent to college, while Mother wasn't. Mother hated her sister for all of that. Supposedly, she liked one of her two brothers, the lawyer, the one I couldn't stand.

Mother told us, her three daughters, many times that "the only people you can trust are your sisters." A penetrating hypocrisy. We sisters were not supposed to be jealous of each other or competitive. Mother's dictum led us wrong, certainly me, then to painful revelations later. People are competitive. You may be committed to socialism, say, but your primitive ego is not.

Over those eleven years Mother transformed, and looked like a picture-perfect little old lady, with wrinkle-free, pinkish skin. As she aged, she smiled more, herself disarmed, maybe, by her illness. She was taking Paxil, a drug that counteracts social anxiety. It helped some, not all of the time. Also, I saw her differently. With her neurological condition, she wasn't the person who had raised me. She was also incapable of being a mother, good or bad. She was mostly benign and not aggressive to me.

When I stayed with her on weekends, though, my depression became acute, I became very sleepy, almost paralyzed with exhaustion. I couldn't keep my eyes open. In her comfortable two-bedroom corner apartment, with great views, east, west, north, and south, I would watch TV, read and write comments on student stories, but mostly I would clean. I don't understand it but I kept her house spotless. I would sit down on her couch, notice a small smudge on the floor, get up and clean it, and sit down again. I was doing it for her, or for me, consciously and unconsciously, keeping her house as she had kept it. Also, by keeping it clean I was creating order against the chaos that her illness had caused, and the turmoil I felt around her.

Mother and I both loved movies and tennis. When young, she went to the movies as often as she could. She was athletic, rode horseback and played tennis, and was good at it. She was strong. As a child, I used to watch her play tennis, and then took up tennis, too. When the U.S. Open was on TV, we'd watch it together. Our best times were watching movies or tennis. If I wasn't at her apartment, I'd phone my sister or her companion to wake her, get her in front of the TV, to watch the Open. Hearing tennis was on, Mother would rush out of bed, get into her chair, and watch all the matches.

Sometimes I imagined I loved her, she loved me. Illusions helped me cope.

I sometimes pretended she was my grandmother. I never really had one, because Mother's mother died when I was two or three; and Father's mother, Rose, was senile when I knew her. She lived until I was eight or nine. My father loved his crazy mother, and Mother hated Rose, because he loved her. My two grandfathers were dead before I was born. Mother was jealous of anyone my father loved. She was especially jealous of his love for his younger brother, Al. My father loved him unconditionally, and Mother didn't ever feel that kind of wholehearted love. I'm sure she didn't.

✦

By the sixth or seventh year, I felt more put out, resentful, and wanted Mother to enter a home. The costs of keeping her at home were not just financial. The weight of responsibility never lessened. I rebelled inwardly. My analyst had often said a good home would keep her in touch with other people like her. She'd have something of a social life. But Mother disliked old people, she said. She never had many friends.

By the eighth year, I thought it was impossible, it would never happen, how long could she live, anyway. I was tethered to this existence finally, and she, and it, was integrated imperfectly into my life, without thinking about it or her. Through all those years, though, it was as if it had just happened. That's the weirdest bit. It was never a regular life. That would return only after she was dead.

Ambivalence, anyway, lived in me—also about placing Mother in a home. I wouldn't want that for myself. And there was some ancient-image-comfort in picturing her at home watching TV or reading, a mother at the ready like one of those cloth-covered, fake monkey mothers provided to baby rhesus monkeys. Scientists had wanted to see if these infants would grow up normally, without an actual mother. They didn't, they didn't learn to behave like monkeys, they weren't socialized, because they had hugged inanimate mothers. Their lives were destroyed by a terrible experiment whose results would seem evident without it.

✦

Around the sixth year, Frances appeared less satisfied, generally, or more discontented with her life, or both. Right, this isn't great work, it's hard taking care of an elderly, sick person. I thought I understood, but my understanding didn't matter and didn't affect her frustrations. We sisters encouraged her to get her high school diploma, study for the equivalency test, so she could get better work. She had had scant education at home, marrying and bearing her first child at fifteen. She studied, passed the language test, failed the math test, then stopped studying. When I encouraged her to take the exam again, she announced, peeved, insulted, "I like myself as I am." I said that wasn't the point, and she walked away from me. Her expectations for herself no longer jibed with her work, but she was not qualified for anything much better. I never mentioned it again.

Any action I took had unknown, unintended consequences, some good, some bad.

There were tensions, predicaments. Sometimes she wanted more time off, a night here and there, and we would usually be accommodating. One time, late in her years with us, she made a plan, without telling me in advance, and wanted time off that night. I couldn't change my plan to suit hers, and she became very angry. It was actually the first time I had said no to her. My niece had finished her PhD thesis, and I was going to her party. Frances was furious with me, and compared herself with my sisters. There it was, the dissonance: She was and wasn't part of the family. It was always about that, in some sense.

Frances's life became less unfamiliar or familiar, while simultaneously more complicated and charged, her needs and feelings more difficult or inchoate to comprehend. Her expectations for herself changed, and also for the job. Some were reasonable, others not. She misplaced her false tooth, having taken it out of her mouth on a train ride with Mother to North Carolina. There they would stay two weeks with my sister and her husband. It was a partial vacation for her, because they took on a lot of Mother's care.

Frances asked my New York sister to pay for a new tooth, because she had lost it on the job. When my sister told me, I couldn't believe it. Couldn't believe she expected that. Frances thought she was owed it, like Workers Compensation, because she'd lost it while doing her job. Probably this became another grievance, another resentment she had against us in a growing list, because we refused to cover it. Her expectation of it, that it was due her, opened a wide door for me to see her different assumptions—what was owed her. "What was owed her" has psychological implications, and they became heavier and more obvious. Who were we to her? What did we owe her?

Frances was good for Mother, even if gradually I felt I

222

didn't really know her. Through it all, I liked her. Frances was in so many ways a sympathetic, warm person, who valued family. She sometimes cooked for our small family, and helped create good family feeling, I thought. She herself was a good mother, she loved her children. And Mother, in extremis, had brought us Frances, and Frances brought our small family together more often. Mother's companion nurtured family-feeling.

She loved my mother. I believe she really did. Her actual mother had remarried a man who abused her, Frances, that's what I understood. Her mother didn't believe her, that Frances was being molested, and they rarely spoke, if at all, after that. I never knew the full story.

It seemed to me Mother had become a mother substitute for Frances. Mother loved Frances. They argued, and Mother could say horrible things to her, but they made up, and love dominated, and that's what counted. It's what guided me, selfishly and unselfishly, and probably misguided me. I didn't see and didn't want to see Frances's flaws, I didn't want her to have a bad character, I wanted to believe in her. Like the nasty neurologist, I refused to consider I was wrong. I didn't want to.

Frances's past was troubled, I learned from her, and her present, which included us, was troubled, and she became trouble for us, more erratic. Some years after she learned of her husband's betrayal, she started wanting a man in her life. She was a healthy woman, with desire and a wish for love.

She found a man, maybe online. She fell in love, hard. She was crazy about him, obsessed, and when he ghosted her, she went mad. The phone bill, the old annotated kind, showed that, for a time, she called him every minute, literally, and each call went into voice mail.

My New York sister told me, again, Frances was taking things from Mother. It was terrible even to consider, and I still couldn't accept it. I didn't want to believe it.

But Frances remained a stalwart companion to Mother, taking her places, staying active with her. I would remember earlier aides who did nothing. It's not a great job, it's on repeat, it can be suffocating and dull. Some people work hard to help their charges, and others do it with no concern for them.

Mother always pointed out how much younger she looked than any other old person. "Looking young" was crucial to my parents, then to their daughters, a plague for life. She and my father appeared much younger than they were, especially my father. His hair remained thick and black into his late sixties. His friends were jealous in a good-natured way, and teased him about dyeing it. He didn't. Once Mother saw a picture of me in a newspaper, accompanying an article about a new novel. She disparaged the photograph. "You look much younger than that." She didn't care about what had been written about the novel.

When she moved to Florida, Mother read airport books, like Sidney Sheldon, which was what the other women in the condo did. She had never read books like that before. Back in New York, and when she was ill but her condition was somewhat better, we would give her books, and she'd read them, but had no memory of what she was reading.

She read James Frey's memoir *A Million Little Pieces* several times. She would often tell me how good it was. She didn't remember what she read, so each reading was new to her. That fascinated me. James Frey and I were once in a spelling bee together, a benefit for the Council of Literary Magazines and Presses, and I told him how she read it again and again. I also told him Mother hated my novel *No Lease on Life*, because it used "bad language." She didn't mind those in his book, I told Frey. When I asked her why, she said, "Because he has to use them." Curiously, while Mother was reading Frey over and over again, the arguments and "scandal" about his book not being really "true," not really a memoir, were raging. Truth or trueness rests only in facts, seemingly, not in verisimilitude.

Oprah's outrage was televised. Frey appeared on Oprah's show, and she asked about his girlfriend's suicide. Did she hang herself? No, Frey said, she hadn't hung herself in the shower, but she had taken pills. Oprah was shocked, horrified. The book had lied to her. The truths in fiction, in representations of realities, were lost in a fury of thoughtlessness.

I thought Frey had been handed a lousy deal, by his agent and publisher. To Mother, none of this mattered. She loved his book.

Mother made progress, as I noted, she did get better, gained clarity, because the brain heals, finds new outlets, makes new pathways. The brain smartly recovers. Mother didn't become herself—from my POV, a good outcome. Her self could be very nasty.

With lessons, she relearned knitting, and it helped her brain grow new cells. Her knitting was never as good, not nearly as good—she could knit coats and suits—but at least she could do it again. Her teacher, Marlene, who also helped her with painting, seemed to love Mother, doted on her, but was a shady character, that's how I saw her. I never trusted Marlene, and Mother loved her.

Marlene participated in what was called a Knit-Out, held then at the Union Square market. Experts and beginners paraded their sweaters and scarves on a catwalk. Marlene entered Mother in the mix of her other students, from a senior center. I believe Mother was her only "private."

My friend Jane attended one of the Knit-Outs, to watch Mother show her stuff. Mother liked Jane very much, which was unusual, Mother's liking my friends. But Jane made it her business to win her, and she did.

Marlene guided Mother to the front of the makeshift stage, and, after introducing her, Mother thanked her and said, taking the mic as if this were the Oscars, "I owe it all to Marlene." My friend roared with laughter.

Frances said Marlene treated her badly. She came to the house and went quickly, and was paid very well, two lessons a week. She catered to Mother—which Mother loved—but after Mother died, we never heard from her again, not even to wonder how we were doing. She didn't care, she may have hated us. To us, she was disingenuous, but she helped Mother. And Mother loved her.

People do things they don't imagine they can, and later wonder at themselves. Adrenaline, will, stubbornness, blindness, ignorance, you get through. I performed the good daughter, my heart wasn't in it, my conscience was. All of us sisters were goaded by conscience. That's not a terrible thing.

Mother had been the opposite of a loving, caring mother, but my parents must have created an atmosphere for their daughters, even with their neuroses and damaging behavior, which encouraged responsibility, conscience, along with pernicious and appropriate guilt.

About Mother, I never felt guilty. Anything I gave her was more than she deserved. That sounds awful. I wanted to behave as I wished she had toward me. Or was caring for her to honor my father, whom I loved regardless of his desperate defects. Or I needed to be honorable. And I didn't feel I could do otherwise.

She sometimes told me she loved me, and she never had before. I remarked to friends on the irony that, after my mother's brain was damaged, she loved me, but really she was incapable of anything but self-love.

She hated my getting attention for my writing. An out-of-town literary critic and friend visited Mother and me. I was in charge of her that weekend. Unfortunately, he instantly talked me up, what a great writer, and wasn't Mother proud of me?

Mother set her dark eyes on him. The critic had a very long, fuzzy beard. She asked him why he had such a horrible, bushy beard. Why didn't he cut it? It was awful. She insulted him for about ten minutes. A good-natured son of a southern minister, he handled her, but I was upset, embarrassed. She had always embarrassed me. At home in Woodmere, she kicked my friends out of her car because they were chewing gum. I was ten. She had a terrible reputation among my friends, this blunt, tactless woman.

Now, for my friend-critic, her performance, her scorching him, because he had praised me, was fascinating, one more piece of why I became a writer. I almost pushed him out the door. Then said nothing to Mother. There was nothing to say.

Before her illness, she cloaked her feelings better—criticizing or rebuking me about all kinds of things, but not openly showing her specific grievance. When she was ill, and before then, if someone mentioned my writing, she would interrupt, "Lynne, when are you going to publish my cat story, about Griselda?" She wanted attention for her writing when mine was mentioned. So, it was obvious, praise for me aroused her demons. I'd tell the visitor how good her story was, and, though it was unfinished, I told her one day I'd get it published. Then she would be mollified.

Mother's story started:

"We had been visiting friends in New Jersey, and when we were saying our goodbyes, my friend said to me, 'Helen, do you like animals—I mean, cats—you see, dear, our neighbor's cat has just had a litter of kittens and there is one darling speckled that looks so sad-eyed and forlorn that I wondered if you could give it a home.' I hadn't thought about cats or kittens for very long time but suddenly there crowded in my mind forgotten memories of my childhood. There was always a cat or kitten in my background . . .

"How could I say no to this furry gentle bundle—I loved it upon sight and so did the youngest of my three daughters who was exactly three. She took the kitten and held it close to her bosom, almost purring in the same fashion as did the kitten. My husband, however, hated cats and although he went along with the adoption, had a long period of reeducation to endure before he too could love the kitten as we did . . .

"The ride home from New Jersey was uneventful and our little kitten found itself very much at home in Ruthie's lap. She petted its head continuously and lifted it up in her little arms to admire again and again, but the kitten, even though it was being lovingly molested, snuggled ever closer without complaint. We knew then we had a precious pet . . .

"By now we had learned our animal was female and in our home predominately female we had one more. My husband alone was masculine, and feeling deprived of male companionship had occasion to say, 'Even our cat is a girl.'

"Each of us had a hand in helping train and teach Griselda little cute tricks but none of us had the persistence Ruthie had for when she determined her kitten learn a new trick it was accomplished. With pride we can say she answered to her name, played dead, draped herself around our necks like a fur piece and followed me to the various markets and food stores whenever I cared to have her come along. She could spot our car from the distance and fly to meet us when the family returned from some trip. She was most unusual . . ."

In the story of six double-spaced typed pages, Mother focused on Griselda's first litter. She writes that "we had over-domesticated her" and Griselda wouldn't give birth without our help. The kittens wouldn't come, and Mother was frantic, and even called a veterinarian to the house. He helped with the first kitten, then left. Griselda's next was breech, and Mother had to pull the kitten out. She stayed up all night with Griselda, very anxious, very worried. Griselda had six kittens, and was a good mother to them.

Here her story ends, her unfinished tale of an astounding cat. I don't know why she never finished it. I may have asked her. She may have answered, but I don't think so.

One reason I am including these paragraphs is that there is something strange, actually uncanny, about the names in the cat story. Mother calls herself "Helen" and me, "Ruthie." Now, without knowing about Mother's cat story, when I wrote *Haunted Houses*, my first novel, one mother is named

Ruth. In my third novel, *Cast in Doubt*, a young female, a mysterious character, is called Helen. I used "Ruth" because of "ruthless." And "Helen" because of an interior decorator who helped Mother choose furniture and wallpaper for our Woodmere house. I watched and listened to her as she talked about design. I was impressed by her. I was about four then.

Also, I believe the woman who cared for me when I was little might have been named Helen. But it is uncanny that Mother chose those names for me and her.

I had respect for her smarts or canniness and practicality. She was smart about illness; dispassionate, she took good care of me when I was sick, she was never "hysterical."

I was eight years old when my parents and I drove to Florida, Miami Beach. My father loved driving. He went home after two weeks, and we stayed on another month. Mother and I saw a Hans Christian Andersen movie in an Art Deco theater, one of Miami's glories. In the lobby, she bought me a collection, ten little books in a box, Golden Books, perfect for an eight-year-old. We took a train home, she booked a comfortable sleeping car, with a bunk bed, Mother slept on bottom, I had the top. The trip would take at least twenty-four hours, I think. But going through Georgia, the conductor went much too fast and missed a signal: Up ahead, there was a hot box, a broken train car, stopped on the rails. Our train should have diverted, but the conductor hadn't seen the signal, and was traveling over 90 miles an hour. He couldn't stop when he saw the broken car. So, in the middle of the night in Georgia, our train crashed into it.

I awoke with a bump, startled, and Mother said, firmly, "Lynne, get dressed, we have to leave the train." So I did. When we were outside the train, I saw fire ahead. A woman was screaming, "Watch the electrical wires, you'll get electrocuted." Mother said, "Don't listen to her. She's hysterical. Don't listen to her." So I didn't.

Three people were killed, including the conductor. The train stayed in that spot for many hours, but they let us back onto the train. They fed us a meal of beef stew, whose smell, if I smell it, still disgusts me, and, during that time, between the train cars, I read my Andersen books to some of the younger children gathered around me. During this time, Mother stayed calm—her best attribute, calm in a storm. She often caused crazy storms, and the ones she didn't, she handled well.

As I said, Mother was practical. She ordered toilet paper and other necessities in bulk, because she told me, when as a child I was curious and asked, she didn't want to be bothered shopping for them. I noted that, and credited her.

She didn't flinch at blood, my father did. She once pushed her hand and arm through the glass part of our back door. Blood gushed. Mother had to drive herself to the hospital, my father in the passenger seat, because he was faint. I take after my father that way. They must have been fighting, otherwise why would she have fiercely pushed open the door and shattered the glass.

Mother used the dictionary and was a ferocious Scrabble player. My nephew was an undergraduate at Columbia University, and Mother invited him to dinner once a week. They played Scrabble, but neither could accept losing, both incredibly competitive. And, ultimately, they had to agree to stop playing.

I learned to love cats from Mother. She was caring and gentle with them. When I was nine or ten, I discovered a litter of kittens and their mother under a bush. It was winter, snow on the ground—I can remember the nearly bare bush they lay under—they would die in the cold. They were outside the temple my family rarely if ever attended, and only on high holidays, if then, for only a year or two. Then we stopped completely. My father was agnostic, Mother an atheist.

I knocked on the temple door, and a keeper answered. He would have nothing to do with helping the cat and kittens. I was horrified, and soon after, stopped believing in God and, in a way, religion, generally, because religious people didn't have hearts.

I phoned Mother, and she drove to meet me with a cardboard box and towels. We rescued the mother and her kittens and brought them home. I can still see them in their box on the floor of the kitchen. The mother cat nursed her kittens until they could be adopted. For that rescue, I loved Mother. Or respected her, if respect can be an emotion.

In the mid-1950s she invited her Black friends into our suburban home. We lived a northern segregated life. Without comment, Mother did it. This may be apocryphal, but I remember hearing that, when I was a baby, my parents took a car trip south. Our maid, who was Black, who may have been called Helen, and with whose son I played, accompanied us to care for me. On the road, we stopped at a place to eat. They wouldn't allow Helen into the restaurant, so my parents ordered food and we all ate in the car.

I admired or respected Mother for several reasons.

Handling Mother's body violated her and me. I remember the first time I took her to the bathroom, set her on the toilet, then wiped her behind, as she called it. Washing her genitals, washing under her breasts, touching her breasts, betrayed the blood tie, and an unspoken order—transgression, finally. When Mother used a commode, carrying it full from her bedroom to the toilet and dumping it disgusted me. I would gag, and that never stopped.

These small, benevolent invasions of her body were weird and discomforting, she was a sick, old woman, her soft skin thinned to tissue paper, coming away from her skin when handled, and she let me handle her. Still, she was my mother, and any feeling I had about her and her place or position in my life might shift and did, but it never entirely shattered. It's what people always say, But she's your mother. You have only one.

Now with blended families, you might have a few. Then you could say, She's my only birth mother. Maybe that will help future generations, or confuse everyone more.

One time, the Carolina sister was staying with Mother during a period when Mother was lying in bed much more and resting longer in her lounge chair. The Carolina sister always paid expert attention to Mother's body; she studied it in a way I never did. Mother said her back was hurting, the Carolina sister asked where. Mother indicated her lower back, her coccyx, which was hot to the touch. It turned out to be a bed sore, an infection invisible to the naked eye. If the Carolina sister hadn't recognized the problem, the infection could have spread and killed Mother.

Over time, except about emptying her commode, I lost most of my compunctions. In the early days, I dreaded taking her places in her wheelchair, going on a bus with her: she was able to walk but her balance was poor. An accident might occur, and she was my responsibility. One time, soon after a shunt revision, I was in her apartment, alone with her, and let her stand by herself, which she was supposed to do as therapy, exercise. To stand and hold on to a windowsill. I turned away for a second, then saw her falling backward like a board onto the hardwood floor. I dropped to my knees, crying, horrified she might have injured her bandaged head. I started crying before I knew it, something that affirms William James's theory that feeling comes before words for it. Mother looked up at me, I was crying, and said, "I'm fine." She also said, "What are you crying about?" Her eyes wide open, she looked at her youngest, as she often referred to me, as if her youngest were crazy. I was terrified.

Mother didn't have osteoporosis, she had taken hormones, was physically strong, walked fast all her life, and, though she fell maybe ten times in as many years, she never broke a bone. She ate healthily, always. Drank almost nothing, and when she did smoke in her forties, and found herself waking up coughing, she stopped just like that. She was healthy, good genes. We ate well—no fried food. My father was an early and avid reader of Adelle Davis.

In the early years of her dependency, I felt self-conscious wheeling her around, like a teenager with her mother at a party. There was an added, ungainly dimension: I had her smile, her pointy chin, though mine was more pointy, her high forehead, though mine was higher. I would become old and decrepit like her, people could see that, my future showed in her. Sometimes Mother blurted weird, personal, mean things in elevators or restaurants. She didn't know what she was saying. The inhibitors in her brain, under pressure, had died.

The other side of this Mothercare account—Fathercare—was Mother's relationship to her husband, my father, and her care of him when he was sick.

Her first cousin Louise once told me, "Your mother loves your father too much." I was startled, a novel, unknown interpretation of Mother. I had just met Louise, or re-met her, and we were on a plane together back to NYC from Florida. Maybe we were visiting my parents at the same time. I don't remember, one of those vague times in the mind.

From childhood Louise had been a close friend of Emmanuel Radnitzky, Man Ray, and they remained friends as adults. Because of this, I believed Louise was sophisticated. Though they were first cousins and grew up together, later Louise and Mother rarely saw each other. To Louise's family, we were the "rich Tillmans," capitalists. Her husband was a taxi driver; for a long time my father, and his brother, had a successful business. (I would call them "accidental capitalists.") Man Ray photographed Louise, but I never saw the work. Louise was beautiful. I liked her and wished I knew her better.

In the 1960s, my father had two heart attacks within six

months. The first was minor, the second major, and a continuation of the first, his doctor said. Both times the heart attack occurred on a Monday morning, both times in an office where he was working.

Daddy was in his mid-fifties. His beloved younger brother, Al, his business partner, had died two years before from a heart attack. Uncle Al had been prescribed Dexamyl by his psychiatrist, Dr. S., long dead, who told my uncle that his chest pain was psychological. Uncle Al died in the hospital that same week.

Uncle Al told my father to take Dexamyl, also, to give him "pep," and a friendly druggist gave Al huge bottles of speed, which he shared with my father, which my father then encouraged me to take, for pep. He gave me a capsule every morning, and I developed a habit before I knew what one was.

In the 1960s, heart conditions were much less controllable or treatable than they are now. Quadruple bypasses were new, rare. My father's cardiologist was considered the best in his field. They didn't know much, but Dr. F. kept my father alive.

He had his second and major heart attack in 1965 or 1966. Mother relied on her eldest daughter to help decide his fate: my father's second heart attack happened in New Jersey, where he had accepted a job with another textile company. He was miserable at it. With his second attack, he was taken to a nearby small Catholic hospital not equipped for a serious heart problem.

The grave question for Mother was to move him, or not, by ambulance to his heart doctor at Mount Sinai in Manhattan. He might die if moved. He would have died if he had stayed in that hospital. Mother decided it had to be done, and he survived the ride. I remember being told that the nuns slapped his hands when, agitated, he twisted his sheets and exposed his genitals. I think he told me, but I'm not certain.

After the second and worse heart attack, it was decided he could use a good rest, in a quiet place. A house in Westhampton was rented for a week or two. He loved the ocean and beach, and I would stay with him. I'm not sure who decided this, other than I was in college, had disposable time, and maybe Mother had a job or other commitments.

In Westhampton, I was my father's companion, the only time I was given that responsibility. I may have still been on Dexamyl, I think I was—I didn't kick until the summer after college ended—because night came and I lay there, hearing the ocean's rhythmic waves, and didn't sleep. I remember looking up and seeing molecules of oxygen.

It was fall, I think, not cold, brisk, nice out. I don't remember much of our time there. I was chewing gum like mad, sugarless and in different flavors, very anxious always.

My father looked wan, his chest a pasty color, and that worried me. I was used to him robust. We didn't fight, when usually we did. We drove into town for dinner, and a movie. The days were calm. I suppose I was reading, and he was, we took walks.

The last day arrived, Mother arrived, opened the door, walked into the Westhampton house, and saw my father and me looking happy, I guess. She began an argument. She couldn't stand it, seeing my father and me together, and discovering we'd had a good time. My father's face settled into sad resignation. Then we all went back, were driven back, but I forget by whom, and whatever good the week had done for him, I suppose, dissipated. Maybe his organs had some healing time.

Until 1981, my father didn't have any further events or incidents, then it all came down. Mother did the grunt work of caring for him during the years between 1981 and 1984, when he died. She kept watch over whatever incident might occur. One day, when opening the door to leave the apartment, my father slurred his words. She said, "You're having a stroke." They went immediately to the hospital.

After he died, Mother rarely mentioned him, not to me, anyway. I didn't see her cry about him. I believe she missed him. She said so a few times. She lived twenty-two years after him. When she was ill, during those years, she said he was a good lover. That was exceptionally surprising.

✦

If he was present and on her mind, she didn't say. In her few notebook or diary entries I found, he made no appearance. But the cat, Griselda, yes.

From a second and only other yellow lined notepad, she wrote in her spidery hand:

"I awoke at 2:30 a.m. with but one thing on my mind— Griselda. So many years had passed and I still think of her. How do I get her out of my mind? Surely there have been other house animals who have preyed on the minds of other people but I know of little in that regard. My thoughts were pleasant but I could not afford to be robbed of much-needed sleep. Wasn't it Shakespeare who wrote: 'Sleep heals the . . . [I can't read the word] sleeve of care.' I continued to think of how unusual an animal she was."

(The sentence is from *Macbeth*: "Sleep that knits up the raveled sleave of care." Perfect that "knits up" is its verb, though Mother, the lifetime knitter, forgot it.)

It's fascinating, and also strange, to me that Mother wondered about "still thinking" of Griselda. She had given her beloved cat away, because Griselda had killed my parakeet. I was just eight. Our unusual cat had opened the closed door to the large den, by turning the doorknob. My ice-blue parakeet had been set free to fly there.

I discovered my pet parakeet headless on the floor. I suppose I was upset, and crying. I don't remember that, only the aftermath. Mother drove Griselda to a shelter, the

Bide-a-Wee home, maybe the next day. I have no memory of being told she was going to do this, maybe I was. It was traumatic for the Carolina sister, who loved Griselda, and for me. And, worse, it was my fault. My parakeet's death caused by Griselda was the reason she was abandoned to a shelter.

At the shelter, Griselda ran out of her cage and somehow out the front door and raced into the street or highway. She must have wanted to find her way back home. I used to hope she'd been found and had a new home. But most likely she was killed on the highway. Imagining her alone and miserable, missing Mother, who delivered her babies, and whom she loved, and on that highway remains a deeply disturbing memory. It doesn't stop feeling raw, a punch in the gut.

No wonder Mother was thinking about her, though she didn't write about her anguish at giving her cat away, maybe having repressed the memory. Her perfect cat remained perfectly happy with her.

In all of Mother's notes, she never suggests any conflict about or sadness with anyone. Everybody always had a great time. She may have thought she was writing the life of a gentlewoman, maybe it was how she fantasized her life. In her writing, at our gatherings we laughed and smiled, and played happy families. She does note her own forgetfulness until she can no longer function well enough to write.

✦

Some friends have had to care for both of their parents. Sometimes sequentially, sometimes simultaneously. We didn't have that burden, my sisters and I had it easier.

When my father was ill, he had my mother. We had relatively little involvement in my father's care, because Mother did that. We rushed down to Florida when there was an emergency, as there was in 1981, when he nearly died—pretty much everything bad that could happen to a heart did. His lungs had filled with fluid, congestive heart failure, his heart was beating irregularly, he had a heart attack.

Sisters and Mother sat in the waiting area all night long. When at last the doctor came out, he told my New York sister, "We thought we lost him, when his eyes rolled back into his head." She looked about to faint, her knees buckled. They had kept him alive, though, at least through the night.

In the morning, maybe six o'clock, I saw him lying on his bed in the Coronary ICU, his face pink and swollen, flush. He was very happy to be alive. He moved his hands, he waved to me. I kissed his head. But his chances weren't great. My father wasn't a candidate for a pacemaker, his heart beat too fast, tachycardia.

Somehow we transferred him to the Miami Heart Institute, I don't know how, or who had the contact to the team there—maybe my New York sister; she had many good contacts. It was meant to be as good as Michael DeBakey's team at Houston Methodist. They pulled him out of heart failure,

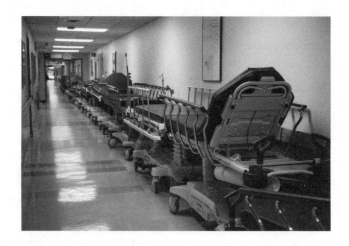

and put him into an experimental group, testing a new drug
to control the beat of the heart—amiodarone. It kept him
alive for three more years. Pretty miraculous, given the state
of his heart—he was living well, not at all limited, with just
18 percent of it functioning, the rest was scar tissue. His doctors called him the Miracle.

Mostly, those last three years, he was in good shape. After
his near-death in 1981, he jogged with weights on his ankles.
He kept in good shape. When the end came, it came fast.
By the time we two New York sisters arrived at the hospital,
he was brain-dead. Mother's friend said, He'll be like this
for a long time. I'll drive you back. So we went back to their
apartment; then got the call to return. He's dead, they said.

But the point is, he was Mother's job. Mother cared for
him. One time when she decided to come to New York, and

stay with my sister, and left him alone in Florida, my father went to some fast-food joint and ate food with a lot of salt, and landed in the hospital. Mother was called, and had to fly home immediately. She was about twenty-four hours away. He needed her.

When a marriage or couple is extant, one of them is supposed to care for the other—if married 'til death do us part is in the contract. Mother liked having him all to herself, even though she didn't want to be in Florida. There, though, my father acceded to her need for his full attention. They fought less. When we daughters were around, her jealousy was like a wild horse, rearing up.

Every year, after she was well enough, we celebrated Mother's birthday with a party. Her last was her ninety-eighth. The first one was her eightieth, when she was fine, healthy, and just before she moved back to Manhattan.

The eightieth was a surprise party, held in my New York sister's spacious apartment. We invited everyone we could. Her favorite brother (one was already dead) came, but her older sister, who lived in Florida, blond and blue-eyed and very arthritic, didn't. Nephews and nieces came. Mother's old friends, alive and kicking, one from as long ago as grade school, who led the sewing class Mother loved attending. Other old friends, people she'd known from living in Brooklyn with her young family. A first cousin I'd never known about or met appeared with her creepy professor husband, who was arrogant and indifferent to Mother and everyone.

Mother opened the door, entered the apartment, and everyone shouted, "Happy birthday." She stopped dead in her tracks, stunned. Maybe she'd drop to the floor, I thought. She looked close to it. I'd never seen her at a loss, she was holding her stomach, and staring. Close to tears, I think. Even when my father died, she sucked it up. I didn't see her cry.

I will never again throw a surprise party.

While she was in our care, after she recovered enough from her surgeries, we celebrated her birthday with a party— ticking off 1997, 1998, 1999, 2000, 2001, 2002, 2003, 2004, 2005, and 2006. We went all out, progressively, and designed the next to be better than the last.

The first was particularly difficult, the lead-up to it crazy, and it was my fault. Looking over her apartment, I saw that her couch looked beaten up, needed cleaning, really needed slipcovers, and this was not long before the party. I decided to take care of it and ordered slipcovers for the couch, a small club chair, and, almost as an afterthought, had the apartment painted. We hired Ray, the wonderful desk clerk and all-around man, to paint. All of this doing and redoing, the shortness of time, created galloping anxiety. Would everything be done. Particularly, the couch. The club chair. I couldn't complain because I had instigated it, playing the daughter who knew how her mother would want her home to look, spic and span.

The party was held in her apartment five times, I think it was, and with each we ordered more amazing cakes, hors d'oeuvres, fruits, chocolates, wines. A baker from Paris, who wanted to sell echt French croissants, opened a store on a corner near me. He was a one-man operation, also serving French-press coffee, but his oven was downstairs. He ran back and forth, trying to keep up with walk-in customers and orders. Finally he couldn't manage.

He made one of the cakes for Mother's birthday, a large rectangle, a French-style chocolate ganache, magnificent, and we paid $120 for it, much too little, really, even many years ago. He probably undercharged everyone, and went bankrupt. Mother's relatives would talk only to each other, they were our first cousins. Her brother attended two of the parties. At the second one, in her apartment, he was in a wheelchair and fragile. I don't remember seeing Mother and him talking. Maybe they did.

As hosts my sisters and I did what we could to create a pleasant atmosphere, an afternoon from one to four. It wasn't for us, but then hosts usually can't enjoy their own parties. And, also, sometimes you don't have the best material to work with. That was our situation. Fortunately, Mother's old friends from Brooklyn days, Dorothy and Milton, had come back into Mother's life, maybe through these birthdays. I'm not sure, and they attended.

I had loved Dorothy since I was a very little girl. Actually the cat that Mother loved so much and wrote her half-story about came from a litter in Dorothy's neighborhood. By then they were living in South Orange, we were in Woodmere, and that's when my parents and they stopped seeing much of each other. They were also at Mother's last birthday party, but by then Dorothy's Parkinson's disease was evident and affecting her. Still, she rose to the occasion, Milton by her side.

Several of the parties were held in restaurants whose owners knew one of us, most often the New York sister. Those restaurants have vanished. I became the person who did the "social managing," preparing the seating plan and putting place cards at each seat. At one restaurant on the Upper East Side, a small, charming, and friendly place, Mother's rude knitting instructor sat down next to her, ignoring her assignment; it was reserved for a close friend or a relative. I explained, and seated the knitter, who was annoyed, next to a man I knew she'd get on with, which she did, and thanked me, later. I really disliked her.

The seating chart became my job. I was acknowledged to be very good at it, though what that skill indicated was never discussed. But I became sorry for party planners; it is a miserable job.

We sisters moved around the room, or moved our seats,

taking care that everyone was relatively content. There was one man, Mother's next-door neighbor, who suffered from the sin of gluttony. It wasn't that he was obese, he was, but he was compulsive, discourteous, and demanding, like a child having a tantrum. At one party in an Italian restaurant in Soho, he disliked his choices on the menu, carefully curated by us and in keeping with our budget. He ordered a whole pizza. The server was surprised, and I just nodded OK. He ate his pizza in a frenzy, while his well-mannered wife maintained her cool. You do, I do, wonder how some long-married people stand each other.

Mother usually knew what was happening, and was very happy with all of the attention. In her apartment, we would seat her on the nice club chair, and people attended to her. I photographed the parties. It gave me something to do, and a way for me to work off my restless energy, also filling people's glasses or picking up some spillage or taking away used dishes. I stayed in motion. Sometimes a friend or two of mine stopped by, and I wondered what they perceived.

Curiously, I don't remember our family celebrating birthdays, not with any regularity or at all. My sisters and I were born in the summer, one for each summer month, so school parties were out, and we might have been at camp or away somewhere else and had parties there. I don't recall parties for my parents' birthdays or seeing them give gifts to each other. I'm not sure we sisters gave each other presents, or had them from our parents, except erratically. With Mother sick, we established a new routine, and we sisters now celebrate birthdays.

I remember one party Mother planned, a vivid, visual memory. I was turning ten, and unusually hadn't gone to eight weeks of summer camp, only two weeks to Girl Scout camp. The party was on the flagstone patio in our backyard, a surface of slabs of different-colored large slate tiles—dark red, various blues, purple. There must have been a cake. I believe friends brought presents, neighborhood friends. I can't remember if it was girls only or boys also. It was a lovely summer day, mid-August, maybe a Sunday afternoon, yes, Sunday. If my parents gave me presents, I have no recollection, but they must have.

In 2005 Mother began to experience frequent mini-seizures; they became very disturbing and more dramatic in July 2005, when she was at my sister's house in North Carolina. Mother visited for two weeks most summers to give us New York sisters a respite, and this sister more time with her. Usually Frances accompanied her, and had a half-vacation; but not this time. Frances had a longer vacation.

The Carolina sister reported that sometimes Mother thought she couldn't speak when she could; said she couldn't talk, then would whisper; that she had uncontrollable laughing fits; she thought she couldn't walk, then with help could.

I saw these mini-seizures knock her out for about two minutes. During those minutes, her head dropped to one side, she seemed frozen and couldn't speak. Worse, she knew what was happening, and hated it, and she wanted to die. She wanted to be killed. She told me she wanted to die. Often she asked, Why am I still alive? Each time, rather than cheering her on, at which she would have sneered, I said something like, You will when it's time, your body isn't ready yet, and I'm sorry.

Mother's seizures were unmanageable for months, anguishing and exhausting her. Sometimes they caused her physical pain. Nothing is worse than seeing someone you love or at least feel sympathy for in pain (though once I asked a sadist how she could stand hurting her husband. She said: It's not my body). By the time Mother's seizures were controlled, she was worn down, and she wasn't coming back.

In early January 2006 I understood she was dying, she had less energy, less strength, less desire to do anything. She was leaving slowly, and I watched with curiosity, detachment, relief, and disbelief. I called the Carolina sister and advised her to visit soon. Mother was going to die, I thought, soon. I recall feeling awkward giving my sister this prognosis. I couldn't be positive I was right, and felt like a bad oracle, definitely an unreliable narrator. It's another aspect of the peculiarity attached to caring for someone who is very sick. You make judgments that can be startling and upsetting; but you feel, as I did, I had to tell my sister, to warn her.

I might be wrong but how wrong could I be, she was nearing ninety-eight. I didn't fully absorb it, even when saying it, I was also incredulous. Mother had revived often, she might beat death again. It's a common delusion—they'll never die—but death doesn't come easily in any sense.

About three months before she died, Mother was sitting at the table, and asked me, "Why didn't you girls put me in a home?" I told her she was adamant about not ever wanting to be in one. Now she said, "That was stupid. You girls have spoiled me."

Weeks before Mother died, my New York sister and she went to the theater. Mother did what she could, until the end, my sister always encouraging her.

Many days Mother lay in bed, listless, or slept on her ugly but serviceable La-Z-Boy chair. In Chantal Akerman's last film about her failing, dying mother, *No Home Movie*, she set up a long shot of her mother lying inert on one of those loungers. From a distance, I thought, she could have been my mother, anyone's mother. From a distance, the body in the chair was generic, an old, sick person, a dying person.

Mother was not doing anything, maybe watching TV, and falling asleep watching. No knitting, painting, going out, no exercise or singing lesson. Her life was drawing down fast. She was existing, only that.

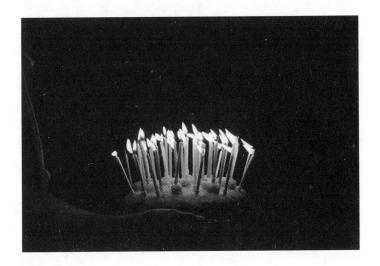

We decided, anyway, to mark her ninety-eighth birthday, which was March 30, and had the party. On the morning, Mother couldn't get out of bed, didn't want to, or maybe just wouldn't. She was speaking very little. She couldn't be awakened.

People were waiting in the living room. We had gathered

a group, many fewer than in years past—her first cousin, brother, sister, her sewing instructor friend, others, all had died. With coaching and urging, and I'm not sure who did it—probably Frances—we managed to dress her.

Mother came out, walking slowly, escorted by Frances or one of us—strangely, I can't remember the details. It was a victory of sorts, a sad one. She seemed to be asleep still, or in a hypnagogic state, out of it.

Mother, seated, still wasn't talking. She seemed to take in that friends were there, though I don't know in what sense. We sang "Happy Birthday" to her, raising flutes of Champagne, and she smiled a little. Then, when the song was over, whether we asked her what she thought or felt, or she just spoke spontaneously, she said: "Sing it again." So we did. That was the last party.

About six weeks before Mother died, I was awarded a Guggenheim Fellowship. I'd applied many times, and been depressed every time I lost, the way many artists are, but finally it happened. I write this because I told Mother. She was doing well, sitting up in bed, clear as a bell, she'd say, and here was good news.

Leaning against her pillows, Mother threw out her arms. She sang out, That's wonderful. What an honor, and so on.

She was dramatic, operatic. I thought, She knows what the Guggenheim is.

About a week or two later, same scene, again Mother was lucid, sitting up in bed, while I sat on the edge of her bed.

She said, out of nowhere, as it's always said, but it wasn't, "If I had wanted to be, I would have been a better writer than you."

"Mother, it's not so nice to be competitive with your daughter."

"I am competitive," she said, and looked at me. I'd say her look was defiant.

I didn't say anything. Mean-spirited, revealing, pathetic. Nothing to say.

Mother spoke what's called the unvarnished truth.

Mother's final weeks return as images. There was much silence.

Mother developed pneumonia in one lung, and one night was taken to an emergency room in a nearby hospital, where young doctors, interns, wanted to cure her of it. She also had shingles on her face that had turned into a painful facial neuralgia, but the doctors didn't want her to have painkillers. They wanted to monitor what was going on with her lungs. Clear it up.

I saw an intern sticking a needle in her neck, trying to find a good vein, Mother's veins weren't easy to find. She was squirming, and cried out in pain. I told him to stop, she was in pain. They wanted to cure her of pneumonia, he said. Forcefully, maybe angrily, I told him, "We don't care about her lungs clearing up, we don't want her to have pain."

Through a circuitous route, the Carolina sister discovered there was a hospice unit four floors above Mother's room. The nurses and doctors hadn't mentioned it, one of the first hospice units in the country. We went up there, and consulted with a geriatric psychiatrist, Dr. M., attached to the hospital. We were damn lucky: she came to Mother's aid and ours.

I took notes: Very practical. Recommend: more fluids, because Mother pulled her IV out. She has poor IV access, sticking and prodding very hard [on her]. Aspirating and coughing because of pneumonia. For fluid: port with sub-clavian, big deal for her. NG tube through nose. Feeding PEG tube into stomach, also uncomfortable. For coughing, aspirating, apple sauce, thickened liquids. Very frail. Sero-quel, low-dose Ativan. High-dose liquid Tylenol. Low-dose Neurontin for shingles.

Dr. M. understood that Mother needed to get out of there, and into home hospice care. She knew we wanted to get her home, and she quickly arranged it, which, we learned, was a feat. We were so lucky to find her. Usually home hospice care takes much longer to set up.

It was a Friday, and Dr. M. was going away for the weekend, to a conference, I think it was in the South. We couldn't get Mother out of the hospital, she explained, until Monday. She said she would stay in touch, and she did. She called from the train taking her south to check on how Mother was doing. She was wonderful.

Nothing happens in hospitals over the weekend. I intend never to get very sick on a weekend. A dear friend of mine died over a weekend, in a hospital, because her regular doctor and unit who were caring for her were not there.

So we had to wait, and Mother lay in bed, not talking, in obvious discomfort.

By Monday, Dr. M. had arranged it so that we could bring Mother home with hospice care. I wish we had realized weeks before, once Mother had pneumonia, that Mother could use home hospice care. Frankly, I don't remember when she contracted pneumonia. I don't remember the two weeks before. There was her birthday party, at which she wasn't well, but still made an appearance, and maybe after that she contracted pneumonia.

Now palliative care was the crucial concept. None of her doctors had mentioned its being necessary, but she had been all right at her last visit with Dr. A. Maybe back when she began having mini-seizures, we should have consulted a geriatric psychiatrist. They look differently at an elderly patient. Not talking therapy, but a recognition, for one, of where the body is relative to death. Where the patient is, herself, about dying. We should have contacted hospice care sooner, we were novices at this, and had been given no instruction on what to do when your mother starts dying.

Still, even death acknowledged can be denied, too.

I remember Mother on the gurney in the street, an attendant with her, and us, Frances wasn't there, and the gurney being lifted into the ambulance. The Carolina sister accompanied Mother into the ambulance. It's funny what remains, and usually as a mental picture.

When Mother was wheeled into her apartment, I was there, and when she was pushed into the living room toward her bedroom, Mother looked up and saw two of her paintings on the wall. I believe she took that in, and took in—she was at home, in the familiar. Maybe she did, maybe that comforted her.

Dying at home always sounded "nice" to me, nicer than in a hospital, more humane. Dying at home conjured images of a benign, calm finish, a good way to die, cozy and warm. The dying would be in a familiar setting, and, especially if they were conscious it would help them. It seemed true enough. We also brought home a nurse whom we'd met in the hospital, an emergency hospital RN. To help us with her.

That was a nice image: She was wheeled into her apartment, and I saw her look at two of her paintings, with surprise. It's still a picture in my mind. After that, nothing nice again.

The responsibility of having Mother die at home was of an emotional and psychological magnitude beyond my imagining.

The day after Mother returned home, a Tuesday, I was in Albany, teaching. The geriatric psychiatrist visited her. She told the New York sister, "Your mother is actively dying." I had traveled to Albany thinking Mother had a few weeks, and when I called home at about 5:30 p.m., after my class ended, I learned the doctor's assessment. Mother was "actively dying." The oxymoron stunned me. I thought, I'll leave in the morning, and still went to a dinner at a fellow teacher's house. My faculty friends recognized what I hadn't, or couldn't: I was in shock, probably. They knew I needed to get home. I didn't, but agreed. I remember sitting in my faculty friend's house, and remember nothing, except that I felt their eyes upon me.

Another friend drove me to the Greyhound station. I dimly remember boarding a dark bus. I think it was a quiet ride, I was not thinking, aware of nothing, time was nothing too, then the bus reached the discomforting Port Authority building. It was about 1:00 a.m. I found a cab, I remember entering my mother's apartment. Both sisters were there. The moments crush together.

Frances wasn't around, she didn't want to see Mother die, she said that to me, but maybe something else moved her to leave. Later, the family gave her a good amount of money for her years with Mother. I added more to it, in fact. And, immediately, she had another job. A friend of ours knew someone who needed someone, so she was set. Until it was all unset. But that happened later.

Dying is an activity, the organs go about their task toward entropy, needing time to shut down. The body is active to the end. It is so odd. Without eating and drinking, people can live up to two weeks.

Her cat, Colette, lay by her side. Mother wasn't talking or acknowledging us. She appeared to be asleep. The nurse we hired from the ER kept "cleaning her up," her words, though Mother didn't need cleaning. She had no fluids in her, nothing to clean, no urine, feces, vomit. I saw that Mother was flat. A board, no flesh, no front or back, both the same, stiff as if dead already. The nurse would move her, turn her over. It brought Mother pain, and, when she showed pain, I asked the nurse to lessen it. She said, "Dying is hard."

I spoke to the New York sister, and said she had to go. We fired her when she arrived the next morning. We couldn't

reach the woman by phone beforehand, she had already be-
gun her journey. We told her only when she arrived, and she
was upset, but we had no choice. Her approach was wrong,
terribly wrong for a dying person, punitive. She was paid for
the day and given extra money for a cab home.

Mother wasn't moving or speaking, just breathing, her
mouth was wide open, her head slightly back on the pillow. Her mouth stayed wide open. Mother's second-to-last
words were heard by me, her knitting teacher, and her massage therapist. The two were in her bedroom, talking, and
Mother must have been listening to them. Suddenly, she
said, "Stupid!" Her knitting teacher loved it. "That's Sophie,"
she said, laughing.

Mother's final words were spoken to her cat, still lying
close by her side. The cat was playing with Mother's left
hand: "Be still," she said. Then the cat was.

Dying is primarily invisible like an oxalis's leaves closing at
night. An outward sign is that, closer to death, toes curve
under, as if clenching.

The process is like birth, I thought, but in reverse.

The geriatric psychiatrist had hooked us up with at-home
hospice care, even though we were really late to do it; we

were very fortunate that the psychiatrist had prevailed. Because she had set it up, a hospice nurse visited us on two crucial nights. The hospice nurse left a booklet explaining how people die, the steps toward death, the process, what to look for. She also left a care package—liquid Ativan, morphine, and atropine. Without her help, it would have been so awful, I can't bear to think of it.

I'd never heard of atropine. I thought of the death rattle as an existential fact, a piece of the battle of life against death—maybe I read it in a story by James Joyce—but it was not that at all. The death rattle is unnecessary. The rattle comes from fluid in the mouth that doesn't anymore go down the throat, because as you're dying your swallowing function stops. Atropine dries up the fluids in the mouth, and the rattle doesn't happen.

Dying is hard, in many ways of course, but this rattle wasn't necessary. And that the ER nurse hadn't suggested atropine was wrong, and she was, in a sense, doing harm to Mother. So that was another reason she had to be fired.

My Carolina sister and I set our alarm clocks, and every hour for almost twenty-four, I think, we awoke to keep her from having any pain. I filled the droppers and handed them to my sister, who applied liquid morphine and Ativan to the inside cheek of Mother's mouth. Also, atropine. Mother never woke, likely in a coma, anyway unconscious.

On her deathbed, Mother had no parting words to us,

her children. It happens often, I learned, sustained silence. Books are published of famous persons' last words, profound, witty, silly. Mother said nothing, nothing at all for four days, profound in its own way. Ever since, I have wondered why I didn't ask her, while she was in the first stages of actively dying, what she was feeling, if she was feeling anything. If she wanted to say anything. I didn't, none of us did, I believe.

The words "awe" and "awesome" must have been meant for sunrises, sunsets, and the human equivalent, birth and death. "Awe" sounds like "oh." The words seem especially made for the end. Oh! Aw! Oh!

Watching Mother die, near her, I couldn't move, speak, ask anything, I was in suspension. What occurred before my eyes, a woman dying, was also not occurring. I observed it, her being undone in slow motion. Dying is inevitable, but estranged from anything you know, watching it feels crazy. Death is always unexpected, even when expected, and this all-too-human event remains inevitable, and incomprehensible. You don't believe you're seeing what you're seeing, and you aren't also able to see it. Then it happens.

Each of us sisters took turns talking to her by her bed, alone, if we wanted, and we did. I can't remember what I said. I cried a lot, which was not in keeping with my feelings toward her. Death terrified me, completely fascinated me, I was gripped by the awe-full sublime.

Each of us sisters had a different mother and father. It's remarkable and true that siblings experience their parents differently, and each can say, "That wasn't how he was with me," or "She liked you better," and "We had different parents," the main source of disorder among them. It is confounding to comprehend just how different parental differences can be. Winnicott's good-enough mother might be good enough for one, not the other.

The last breath would come, we learned, fifteen or twenty seconds after the previous breath. She will not be breathing, and then there will be a last gasp for air, or a great exhalation of what air is left in her lungs. We waited for that, doing vigil.

A few days before Mother died, Frances's Catholic church choral director and his two-or-three-year-old daughter, who had visited Mother several times, called on us. He wanted his daughter to see Mother.

In dying her mouth opened wide, her facial expression a rictus, she looked as if she were in pain, though she wasn't. We didn't want the little girl to see Mother this way. My New York sister told him, No, I'm sorry, your daughter can't see Mother. He said something like it was part of their faith to see the dying, and death. My sister said, again, No, we don't want your daughter to see Mother like this. He was very disappointed. I was relieved his daughter wouldn't have this ugly image in her mind.

On Mother's last day, the Carolina sister was reading by her bed, and I was sitting on the end of the bed, watching Mother. The New York sister was on a break, eating breakfast or lunch in the dining room. She never eats much.

I looked away for a second, and, when I looked again, I realized she wasn't breathing, hadn't for many seconds, there was no intake of breath. I ran to the bedroom door and called out to the sister eating lunch, "Come. Now." She literally dropped her plate onto the dining room table, and rushed to the bedroom.

So, we three sisters were by her side when she died.

I set my hand on Mother's skeletal shoulder, and, as she took that excruciating last gasp, one shoulder lurched forward.

She was already in rigor, stiff as a board. Her mouth was agape, and could not be pushed together, her jaw set. I was afraid if it were pushed, forced to close, it would break, crack apart. Her open mouth made her look tormented, like a stone gargoyle in agony, in hell. Her death seemed not to have been, though. When actively dying, her mouth had opened and stayed that way until death.

She died at 1:00 p.m. exactly on Saturday, April 29, Duke

Ellington's birthday. Mother had no pain, none that could be seen during the last few days, and none at her death. My Carolina sister and I had dosed her into a coma.

I can't remember what happened next. Or who called whom; the City's medical examiners were called, they had to prepare a death certificate, and the City needed to remove her body. When they arrived, two small men in identical jackets, they nodded to us, and walked into Mother's bedroom, pushing an empty gurney, with belts on it, the kind familiar from TV and movies, and oddly unfamiliar in this setting. When the two men reappeared, the gurney carried Mother in a body bag, strapped to it. We sisters watched the men do their job almost too efficiently. They wheeled her out of her bedroom, moved quickly to the door, and disappeared, Mother's corpse with them. We saw it, that black rubber bag, for a few moments. Mother was just a thing now, anomalous, an object, nothing anymore. The men's expertise added to her nonexistence. This was done to everybody, anybody, the impersonalness augmenting her new nothingness.

POSTMORTEM

Tempus edax rerum.
Time, the devourer of all things.

—OVID

In early May, we sisters ran an obituary notice in *The New York Times*. We mentioned the names of all of her current aides and helpers, two of her oldest, living friends; so many had died before her. When you live to ninety-eight, that's inevitable. We thanked the staff at the apartment building where she lived, and her doctors by name, internist, neurologist, neurosurgeon, and dermatologist. I wrote the obit, maybe because I'm an obsessive obit reader, and included her savvy response to Welles's 1938 "War of the Worlds" radio program. "Turn to another station."

The neurologist was touched that he was cited and wrote us a letter. He said he appreciated Mother's vivacity and resilience. She was tough, and her doctors respected that. I have a feeling, or hope, the neurologist became more positive and experimental with his elderly patients, but I don't know.

We also planned what I thought of as shake, a shiva-wake, both rituals worthy send-offs of the dead for the living. The gaiety, false or real, of a wake, the comfort of friends sitting in the home of the bereaved, consoled by talk and food, alcohol and jokes—ours was not one or the other, a fusion maybe, or its own thing.

We provided the liquor and wine and food, no one had
to bring anything, though many brought flowers. We invited
friends and colleagues to visit on two evenings, after six. We
didn't need or want to be with people all day long. Doing
the providing, a friend told me, was strange, not the way it's
usually done.

I wanted to show a couple of old friends, one of whom
is a great painter, another a writer, Mother's paintings. Her
massage therapist burst into my group of intimates, and destroyed the moment. Why it affected me so strongly is curious, but I never felt the same about her again. Not being
in control of one's emotions is an answer. But how strange
really, and still it's not the first time that has happened to
me. Years ago, a close friend gripped the back of my neck to
stop me from laughing. Her grip was like a vise, and shocked
me, I did stop laughing—this was at a literary reading, I
was also one of the readers. Later, when she approached and
hugged me I would recoil some. It was involuntary. Years
have passed, and while I like her I still have that reflex or
phobic response.

Death customs—hundreds, thousands of rites, which I
suppose correlate to the structure of feelings in various
cultures and religions. How differently people, of different
cultures and societies, sound when they cry, and how they

cry. Burial conditions, burning bodies, or setting a body into the ground, and in what direction, in a burlap bag or shiny box.

Ours for Mother was simple, no speeches, we had her cremated, and her ashes are with the New York sister. Not that long after her death, not sure of when exactly, I arranged to have tiles made in her and my father's honor, to be set into the ground at Tompkins Square Park. On the day the tiles were unveiled, and other people's were also, friends joined us sisters in the ceremony. Then we invited our friends to lunch at Danal, a now-defunct lovely restaurant in the East Village, where Mother had dined a few times, and a favorite of mine.

Those tiles are set in stone, and there for however long, but not eternity. So there is a place to go and to think about them. To remember people I loved, to mark their having existed, is crucial. I worry I will forget and keep reminders so I won't.

My father died in Florida five days before my birthday. Right after he died, I immediately started making phone calls to funeral homes. I took it upon myself, and no one stopped me. I searched for a home that buried people at sea. I thought he would want that. I phoned several homes, and the voices talking at me put me off immediately. (And, I thought about *The Loved One*.) And none performed sea burials. Luckily, a friend of my father's came to pay his respects to Mother, and told us about the Nautilus Society. It started, I learned, in the 1960s as a "countercultural" way to dispose of the dead.

I phoned the society and a man's voice on the other end of the phone did not sound like an unctuous mortician but a person. We arranged for a cremation and burial at sea. My father had loved the ocean, loved sailing on it, though he became horribly seasick, or as he'd say, "sick as a dog," and went anyway. He loved swimming and swam far out past the breaking waves, always in a parallel relationship to the shore. He was a strong swimmer.

Before his cremation, he was embalmed so that our small family could gather for his funeral. It was a nothing send-off. He lay in his coffin, in a bare, dismal room with chairs, and we, sisters and wife, were there, but none of his friends from "the building," as my parents always referred to them, attended. A first cousin and her family showed up, finally. They were so late we sisters were compelled to read our eulogies again. And then he—I called him Daddy or Pop—was cremated.

My father was a very popular guy, people loved him, and yet there were none of his friends at this nothing ceremony. Maybe we didn't tell anyone. Probably we didn't. I don't know why.

Mother's envied sister didn't show up, even though my

father, every Saturday, would drive an hour to Miami to pick her up and take her shopping. She had no one else. This infuriated Mother, his helping her selfish sister, who, when the man who took such good care of her died, didn't bother to come to his funeral.

Mother, my sisters, brother-in-law, niece, and nephew, we sailed out to sea to spread or bury his ashes. We lounged or stood on a white yacht. The sun was very strong and direct, an August in Florida. Out at sea, each of us sisters, one by one, was handed the urn. I didn't see Mother. She must have. Each took a handful of shards and fine matter, or Daddy, and tossed it overboard. When my turn came, the yacht shifted, rolled some, and I thought I was falling overboard. Unconsciously, maybe, I was hoping to join him.

Funeral rites, ways of mourning, fascinate me. I bought an old anthropological work by E. [Effie] Bendann, *Death Customs: An Analytical Study of Burial Rites* (published in 1930 by Kegan Paul). Anthropologists like to find similarities across civilizations and societies. There are many; the subtle differences are intriguing. In some societies and tribes, fires are kept burning at the head of the buried body. Food is often a part of burial, so that the dead may eat. In Florida, and I don't know in which tribe, the practice was, during the ceremony, to offer food to the dead; someone says, "This is for you." In Melanesia, burial was regarded as a tribute to the ghost. Ghosts, in early societies, were sometimes great, sometimes unimportant. Some stayed around.

After my father died, I couldn't stop crying. I wore a shirt of his to sleep in for over a month. I went into a mourning that hasn't entirely ended. Long after my father died, I felt he, something of him, was lodged slightly above my heart. It was a physical sensation. Sometimes in an old-style southern Italian restaurant, like Lanza's in the East Village, I would order veal parmigiana because he loved it. I would imagine him eating it, tasting it, I could see his face then as he chewed with delight, and felt I was tasting it for and with him. Swallowing was hard.

I didn't grieve for Mother or mourn her. I was stunned with relief and deadened by exhaustion, inducing light-headedness, not giddiness. The pressure of eleven years, Mother, was gone, dead like her. But it, that psychic load, took more time to dissipate. While it felt emotional, psychological, it also felt physical, actual weight, even though primarily nonphysical. Those senses remained, alarmingly in some ways. I often was caught short, imagining I had forgotten something I was supposed to take care of. I'd go to the phone. But there wasn't anything I'd forgotten, except that she was dead. Life was full of reflexes.

✦

We sisters donated her confusing and damaged brain to a clinic whose scientists were researching the aging brain. Mother would have liked that, she was medically interested, like my father. Then, as he was, she was cremated.

An autopsy report is a strange text. The language is strictly medical, for example: "The highest neuritic plaque density is in the insular, temporal and parietal sections, with relatively fewer neuritic plaques in the occipital lobe sections." While I have some scant knowledge of the lobes, and their functions, often forgetting which is which, I need to look up "neuritic" (thinking it's connected to "neurotic"): "Senile plaques (also known as neuritic plaques) are extra-cellular deposits of amyloid beta in the grey matter of the brain."

In every sentence, there are several to many words whose meanings I don't know, and would have to look up; then I don't know what is better or worse, good or bad or neutral, about them.

Mother's report was five pages long. Here is the summary, or "neuropathology final diagnosis":

    1) Alzheimer's disease
    2) Binswanger's disease (vascular dementia)
    3) Subdural hematoma, chronic (bleeding in
    the brain)
    4) Infarction, left occipital lobe, chronic

(blockage of blood; in the heart, a heart attack)

Early on, Mother's symptoms didn't align with an Alzheimer's diagnosis, as I noted. She did get better, relearned
knitting, could read, didn't have complete memory loss, recovered some. Alzheimer's patients do not, they just keep
losing function.

But in the last two years of her life, she slowed down,
more and more, and had less capacity. Maybe the shunt had
worked sufficiently, so that it "cured" or lessened the hydrocephalus. Maybe, with age, her brain was overtaken by other
diseases, Alzheimer's and vascular dementia came to have
greater roles at the end of her life. It seems so.

I found a message I sent to Dr. A., dated June 14, 2004—
and now writing this, I just realized I am writing of it on the
same day but sixteen years later, another coincidence with or
without meaning but somewhat uncanny. The detail in the
letter to her internist shows the vigilance required, or that
we sisters required of ourselves.

Dear Dr. A.,
    Mom sustained the new schedule of sleeping through the
night for two nights after Frances returned, so that means

she had about 12 nights of good sleep—and then she has had three or four "bad" nights—not only didn't she sleep but on the first bad night she was very agitated and angry and thought she was in jail. Then she had three or four bad nights, though none quite as agitated as the first, and then this Sat. Night (the 12th) she again slept well, Frances told me yesterday. Now, my sister called and said last night Mom went to sleep, woke up and didn't recognize Frances. So Frances called her and my sister talked to Mom on the phone and quieted her, calmed her.

Frances says this has been a pattern of hers for a long time now, not sleeping for some days, then doing Ok again. I'm not sure about the non-recognition part, though—she didn't recognize me when I went into her room one night after she'd been sleeping and awoke, because I think she doesn't seem to be able to make distinctions between dreaming and waking life . . . Her brain is a very strange machine these days."

I ask Dr. A. about the med, Paxil, she has been on for a while. I had read that it can backfire, as antidepressants sometimes do, and create other problems. Maybe it should be changed?

These were probably symptoms of vascular dementia or Alzheimer's or both.

✦

We didn't let go of her rented apartment for two months, which angered the building's management. Moving out required our going through all of her things. Decide what to throw away or keep. And who wanted what. I wanted one lamp. I'd asked Mother about it years before she became ill, and my name was written on a tag under its base. It was Chinese, old, carved, shaped like an urn.

We sisters divided things easily, and if there was trouble or difference, it was resolved fast. None of us was that committed to any of her objects, I believe. One or two things, yes. There were her paintings, and we divided those. The garnet ring Mother intended for me was gone. I had wanted it, a cluster of garnets like a bed of purple flowers, but it had disappeared.

So we held on to Mother's apartment until we were forced to leave it. Very unpleasant, but necessary, maybe, to be forced out. We had to let it go. Not just the apartment but what it represented, her life there, twenty years of our visiting her there.

In high school, in my yearbook—I was its "girl co-editor"—the phrase I put under my photo was: "Long Day's Journey into Night." High school dramatic, melodramatic, funny, but I knew the sadness and pain in my family, of its going on and on, and of our agonistic nature.

Mother's killer sentence, "I would have been a better

writer than you if I had wanted to be," was surprising only because she had voiced it. It sounded as if it could have been a line in O'Neill's American tragedy, when the sons argue with each other or with their father.

After her death, I learned that Mother had said the same words to her singing teacher, the massage therapist she wanted to marry, and my friend who was friendly with Frances. They never told me, and I suppose it would have been awkward for them. and what could I do about it, anyway. It wouldn't help me to know then. I don't know how, in that context, I would have responded.

Later, a friend said, "It was good she told you. Now you know you were right." She was very competitive with me. But I'm not sure. It confirmed a reality I knew, but Mother's unrelenting rivalry and her need to tell me, especially that, her need to tell me, was devastating.

I write what's next with some reservations.

In the hospital, before we moved her home to die, I was sitting on the side of her bed. Mother raised her right hand, with difficulty, and stretched her arm so she could stroke my cheek. It took a lot of effort, and then, with a deep sigh, she closed her eyes, and dropped her hand to the bed. All the while we looked at each other, neither of us speaking.

Her tender gesture can be interpreted variously.

✦

Mother envied all of her daughters. She loved my father, whatever love meant to her, to them, and she was jealous of him and of anyone he loved; he could never give her enough, though she'd never admit it.

Her childhood deprivation was more emotional than material, though her family had little money, and I don't know how little. That deprivation of love most likely made her angry, selfish, mean. Her family was harsh, but she insisted she loved her mother. She rarely, almost never, mentioned her father, except to talk about that small wooden box in which he kept his treasures, and no one else was allowed to see its contents. She resented him for that.

She resented her older sister, her blond hair and big, blue eyes, who was sent to college when Mother wasn't. Her two brothers were sent to college. Still, Mother said of her mother, she was perfect. I didn't believe it, this lie she told herself. Someone whose mother loved her, I felt, whose mother was perfect—whatever that might be—wouldn't treat her own children the way Mother did. That's what I thought and think.

I suddenly had more time, time became space, a spaciousness to think and move freely, have my own worries, not about her, and do some writing. I felt extreme relief. Maybe I missed Mother when I was a young child. I must have. But

I went to sleepaway camp for eight weeks, when I was eight, and didn't miss her. Being away from her and a family that was contentious and fighting, living in a new setting with new people, offered a sense of what the future might bring: Freedom. If I could get away. And then I did, years later. I didn't miss Mother.

What I miss, what I can never have, is a good or good-enough mother, a taste of unconditional Mother-Love. Curiously, what I missed after she died was a routine I had never wanted. Routine can be comforting, consoling, because you don't have to think about what you're doing, you do it, it's rote.

I once worked as a proofreader at *Forbes* magazine, had days on and off, and it was always the same in the proof room. Nothing happened in the cramped, windowless proof room that touched on my so-called real life. There were OK days, bad days, and worse ones. It could be gloomy. Arguments happened, annoyances were plenty. But basically, sameness prevailed. That had its advantages, because I left my real problems behind and dealt only with proof-room issues, mostly petty, and which weren't important to me and could be left in the room.

Exposing myself, Mother, a family's inner workings, in this account, is strange to me, very uncomfortable, even disturbing. If I use something that happened to me in a story or novel, the experience comes into it, not my feelings about it. I don't write about myself. This may be hard to understand if you don't write fiction, but it's common. Experience is a writer's material, my material, but I rarely write autobiographically, or about people I know directly. I have strong reservations about doing it, and now I am doing it.

This is a sad story.

When Frances and I were still in touch, infrequently but in touch, I attended a dinner party. A stranger and I started talking, and Frances's name came up. The woman had mentioned an artist for whom Frances had worked right after Mother died. I told her I knew Frances. Then she looked very troubled. She explained, somewhat reluctantly, that Frances had become an aide to a man she knew, a famous Broadway and movie composer. Video evidence existed, showing Frances stealing.

"Frances is a thief," the woman said.

The word "thief" had never entered my mind. Maybe she "took things." That sounded benign. What she took didn't matter, it was little stuff, if she did take stuff. When Mother was alive, even if she were stealing, firing her would divorce Mother from her longtime companion, who was great with her, and Mother loved her. Could Mother adjust to a new person. My sisters and I didn't think so. What was most important—Mother was looked after well, kept safe, loved, and Frances gave her that. Our dilemma and differences caused some tension among us. There was an ethical issue, but right and wrong entangled, and values had to be weighed. I had always defended Frances.

Now this was different. It wasn't my family. I had to tell her current employers, whom I knew. It was the responsible thing to do. What would Frances say and do? Her employers were anguished, they had trusted and depended upon her, and they fired her.

A month later, Frances wrote me and threatened to

inform the government that my family had employed an undocumented worker. Frances didn't attempt an apology or offer an explanation. Whatever her stealing meant—neurosis, a compulsion like kleptomania, because she also took from a mutual friend, impotent fury at her employers—I didn't write her back, there was no point. I didn't know what to say. I told my New York sister I was sorry. Some days everything feels sorry.

At first, writing about Frances, her life, remembering her many years with Mother, I felt anguish again, the pain again. Now, having written the Frances story, that pain has gone, and with it my anger. And I feel a little heartbroken as if what I experienced and came to write is a domestic tragedy, about Frances, Mother, and me.

Tragedy, according to the Greeks, happened only to the well-born, kings and queens. So-called ordinary people, not elevated in life, their mental anguish also wasn't. Their falls weren't caused by hubris. The forces against them weren't as "interesting" or "complex." This prejudice holds.

But very often their endings seem fated, given the beginnings, just as Oedipus's was.

I left something out. I didn't want to mention it. Toward the end of Mother's life, Dr. A., her beloved internist, told me over the phone that Mother had pneumonia; he was treating her for that with antibiotics. I am not sure exactly when he told me. It was a very confusing time, because Mother was at the edge of life. If I knew she had pneumonia, I may have assumed my sisters did, also. It's said pneumonia is an old person's friend, a good way to die. But no one said explicitly your Mother is going to die soon; why don't you look into home hospice care, why don't you prepare for that eventuality.

Thinking back, I believe we should have been told. Doctors treating very ill people should inform patients or patient advocates about hospice care, about end-of-life procedures. I don't mean to "blame" Dr. A., but my account would be inaccurate if I didn't speak to this issue. It would have alarmed all of us to know she was dying, but it would have helped to know how to proceed.

So, not long before she died, Mother was taken, as an emergency, to a nearby hospital. While she shouldn't have been, curiously, it turned out to be a felix culpa. Because she was, hospice care was engaged. The Carolina sister researched the hospital and discovered the unit's existence there. When we realized Mother wasn't going to recover, that the young doctors trying to cure her caused her pain, we took the elevator to the hospice unit, found the helpful geriatric psychiatrist, and she set it up.

✦

Attending to Mother enforced regularity. Usually I want to change up things, often by reading what I don't know about and don't live. I don't look for identification but the chance to disidentify. I walk around the city, wanting some strangeness, and talk with strangers who might become friends but usually don't, but one intense conversation might reset my day or night or mind. I'd say "forever" but that is unknowable.

The problem with a routine is that when you're wedded to it—let's say, it's breakfast, and you must have an egg or your kind of coffee or tea—when that gets disrupted, even temporarily, so you can't perform it, the rest of the day is off, and it all feels wrong.

Now, when I walk up First Avenue over to Second Avenue, which I did consistently for eleven years, to Mother's apartment, I remember the walk there, and what I saw along the way. The pet store with no pets. The two bagel shops near each other. Another bagel store. Slice-of-pizza-with-a-Coke stores, a Thai restaurant, a supermarket, and fruit and vegetable stores. The going-out-of-business signs. The shops across First Avenue where I rarely walked, and the Swiss restaurant where we as a family took Mother once or twice. The medical appliance store in front of which I regularly paused and studied the display.

I like those stores, their show windows. They can't become fashionable unless an artist or window dresser designed the space as an installation of grotesqueries, things without names. Windows decked with anonymous rubber tubes, male and female urinary devices, and hard plastic objects that seem S&M-ready. Packages of gauze in different widths and lengths, bandages, various commodes, and mysterious appliances and appurtenances I hope never to have to use.

Generally, adult diapers are not in windows but on shelves at drugstores and supermarkets. Buying them for Mother at CVS once embarrassed me. People would think I was pissing myself. I was like a teenager buying condoms. Time came, I didn't care what anyone thought.

Wheelchairs in the store window captured me, some looked so flimsy, but I guessed they would suit the very frail, and then there were those for obese people, who would be hard to push. Mother had a sturdy-enough chair, and pushing her to the park was a relatively painless experience. I felt magnanimous, a do-gooder, and so I was not embarrassed: the difference, I thought, was about how one is seen. In movies, people pushing wheelchairs or baby carriages appear to be nice people, worthy. This good image prevailed, flimsy or irrelevant as it might be.

In the park, there were no bad incidents. Mother liked flowers, birds—her mother had kept a canary or two—liked watching children playing. Life lived around her, around all of us, Mother, Frances, me. It could be the Luxembourg Gardens, I'd tell myself, and I'd bring a book, but usually wouldn't read. Being with Mother, I'd feel restless even in a calm place.

Through her incapacitation, the world of handicapped or disabled people became more than evident—vivid, distinct, ever-present. That stigmatized world was everywhere, and I saw "them" differently. Watching people in wheelchairs on the street, people propelling themselves onto a kneeling bus, or speeding by in motorized chairs, people walking with a limp, I recognized their trouble, predicaments, their ordinary challenges. Mother's condition worked like a heuristic device—so many consequences are unforeseen and incidental.

Noticing anyone pushed in a wheelchair, I might glance at the person, most often a woman is in the chair, and the one pushing it, usually a woman. I walk by a woman in a chair, smile, maybe it's a gratuitous gesture, but elderly people usually smile in return. And their caregivers, sometimes. These are consciously performed recognitions—to notice, not to ignore them. When I was pushing Mother's wheelchair, many looked away.

Now I behave more patiently or more compassionately, I hope I do, say, seeing someone struggling to walk. I notice and read strain or grimaces on faces, and watch for people stopping to catch their breath, taking deep breaths, pronouncing great sighs, their mouths wide open. I know they are in pain.

In New York City, these people are not hidden from sight, they are in plain sight, if you notice them. The healthy and capable elderly take buses, go shopping, go to movies, take walks, slowly, go to restaurants alone or with friends, they live among and with us. They live. That's the point.

The turning away interests me, the ignoring, ways to ignore inevitability. Now that I have seen the inevitable, against my will, which I didn't want to see or know, I can rarely pretend it won't happen to me, and pay more attention. Let's say, I have become aware.

Women are caring for women, mostly women of color doing this work, tending to their white charges, pushing the wheelchairs, paid to care for women, mostly, sometimes men, but men usually have male caregivers. I see far fewer men in wheelchairs, still. I always look for differences in that coupling. I also look at the women of color caring for other women's, white women's, children; they are nannies or maids. Cell phones keep them connected now to their friends and families. I'm relieved when I see women pushing what appear to be their own babies.

Death was a longtime fascination. At five, before bed I begged my father to bury me in a coffin with my pillow and blanket, my hands under the blanket, so I wouldn't be cold if I woke up dead. Woke up dead. He said he would. He understood anxiety, he suffered from it.

After Mother died, my fascination was piqued and invigorated, if I can say that, ramped up by having watched it, by coming into contact with terms like "actively dying," and with people around the dying, tending to one after another.

I read Sherwin Nuland's *How We Die*, which detailed all of the facets leading to death, how the organs shut down, how death comes from many causes, though one appears to dominate. The "facts," I hoped, would supply a kind of comfort, though knowledge is not always power. Or, doesn't make one feel powerful.

I decided to investigate hospice care, presumably for an

essay I was commissioned to write for an anthology of writers on death. But I didn't end up using the material for that essay. Hospice, in its contemporary usage, was the idea of a British doctor, Dame Cicely Saunders, who, in 1948, had worked with dying patients around London. Later, in 1963, she lectured at Yale University and told U.S. health care professionals about hospice and palliative care. Many years have passed, and many in the United States still don't get it. Hospice to them means instant death, while the reality of hospice is living longer, and pain-free until you die.

I contacted various organizations with hospice services, and told them I was writing about hospice care for an essay or book; I found three professionals who agreed to be interviewed by me. A head nurse in charge of many nurses, a regular nurse, and a death counselor. I was afraid to meet them as if I would meet death itself. I know, it's ridiculous. Still, being close to them was being very close to death. I met with each in person.

I felt superstitious, daring fate. No wonder there is religion, no wonder there are superstitions. If you cannot know what happens after, and you cannot, belief relieves anxiety about a mystery with no solution to it, only an improbable solution named faith. I'm not sure what I expected. I think I hoped to be released from great fear into a benign fear, a certainty that death wouldn't hurt me, I nearly wrote "wouldn't kill me." The irony is killing. I didn't want to die in pain, and dying in my sleep was preferable, but there would be no time to plan. If I knew I was dying, though, I'm not sure what I'd plan. Not my funeral. When I do imagine my funeral, when I'm very depressed, wanting to die, and also when not wanting to die, I know some people would arise to manage it, but they wouldn't know all of the people in my life, and the fantasy of preparing for it becomes nightmarish and exhausting. Then I'd rather die in my sleep.

I wanted to get closer to hospice workers, to know about their work, to understand what they do, and why, and to demystify them, and demystify dying, which is impossible, even when knowing the biological reasons for it. Not knowing what happens afterward, again, that's the mystery. Looking at Mother dead, I didn't think she was going anywhere.

Speaking with the counselor was particularly vexing. That's hard to explain. I suppose I saw him as the magic bullet, the one who would say the essential, reassuring words to the dying, so that they would go without fear into that dark night. Those words would also reassure me. But nothing he said was magical. I was not placated. Death was still death.

He had been a priest, he told me, but that was something he never told patients, because he was nondenominational in this work.

My wish, unconscious mostly, was to discover what is

impossible to know. How death will be for me. But no one told me what I wished to hear. The head nurse was kind and businesslike, he managed the other nurses, sent them where they were needed, and rarely saw patients. The regular nurse, an RN trained in hospice work, explained what palliative care was, and how she dealt with families. Many worried about the dying person taking morphine and becoming addicted, which is of course very strange, given the person's condition, but relieving their pain was trumped by their relatives' fear of addiction and "morals."

Dying people can suffer horribly because of a family's objections. Make sure that you have written down the name of your health care proxy, and what you want done or not done. A living will it's called, oxymoronic as "actively dying," but maybe anything related to death is connected weirdly.

Like the death counselor, she encouraged them to deal with the "loved one" with honesty, talk with them about what's happening, ask what they want, their wishes, their wills. She told me, often the dying person will die after everyone has left the room. This made sense to me. Dying means leaving everyone, abandoning them, and how can you when they won't leave you.

I would have to wait until I died to know death, and then it would be too late to comfort myself. Another of life's paradoxes. Unless I committed suicide and staged my end, the way the artist Ray Johnson did—he was known as a correspondence artist, his material, letters and postcards which he sent through the mail. He planned his suicide for a year at least, sending postcards to people, intimating something that could not be discerned. A friend of mine, Callie Angell, who received several postcards from him, realized after his bizarre suicide—he was last seen floating in a stream or river flowing to the Atlantic—that he had written messages that intimated his intentions, his decision to die. It perplexed her to have figured that out only later. And, later, when Callie took her own life, shocking all of us friends, I wondered if, among many things, Ray Johnson came to her mind.

I was once told that suicides are people who can't wait to know the end, and who need to control it. Their fate. That must not be true for every suicide, but I understand the concept. Though it is self-defeating.

When both parents have died, people say they feel orphaned. Now I am an orphan, they say. Also, with a strange shock they recognize their generation is next. I didn't feel orphaned, though I like the conceit: with Mother gone, I was now, objectively, a motherless child. I did realize, with dismay, that my sisters and I had moved to the top of the mortality list.

I was about seven or eight when I learned that, in the

Jewish religion, on Yom Kippur, God wrote in a big book; he wrote the names of those who shall live and those who shall die. On that day, observant Jews were meant to recall what they had done wrong and repent, or pray not to be taken. On this special day, often called a holiday, belying its meaning, the religious are supposed to fast to appease God, a kind of sacrifice, a primitive notion, and, also, very last minute.

It fostered an idea in me: suffering served a holy purpose. It was part of the travails of being a writer, and also God was a writer who wanted his people to suffer and who tested them. It anointed the practice with a supreme power. I didn't and don't believe in God, but still I adopted the idea: God was a writer. Who shall live and who shall die, especially. There are some writers who think their work is that important.

On a very early Sunday morning in the house in Woodmere, the phone rang and woke me; I raced to it, set on a little table in the hallway between my bedroom and my sister's. I was sixteen, a new junior in high school.

Sit down, a friend said. I sat down, didn't ask why. She said: Lois is dead. What. She's dead. A car crash.

Lois was my first friend to die, I mourned her for almost a year, not aware of what mourning was, and her death changed my life. I said to myself, Lois died and now I must make my life worthwhile, to honor her. In a way, I stopped acting like a teenager, didn't go to parties, didn't care, stayed home, did my homework, and became an honor student by doing my homework.

My favorite uncle died when I was eighteen. My friend Billy was murdered, his murderer was never found. My near-favorite protagonist, Horace, in my novel *Cast in Doubt*, was based on a man I knew slightly. The man was murdered in a horrible way. I didn't tell that story in the novel, didn't end it that way, it wasn't the story I wanted to tell, which was, in part, about survival—it was written during the 1980s–90s AIDS epidemic. Friends and many acquaintances died then, stripping life of the certainty that everything could be cured.

By now, many people I know have died, some people I cherished, and the frequency chills me and is numbing. I thought I cried easily, but now I don't.

Parents' deaths—they're different, usually. These characters leave the world, and, improbably, absurdly, their children feel shorn of symbolic protection, and, in a sense feel naked and more vulnerable. It's said the worst death is that of a parent burying a child. It disrupts the natural order. The natural order shows itself to be unnaturally painful.

When my favorite uncle lay in his coffin, his ancient uncle, his white beard like an Old Testament prophet's, looked upon him. Uncle Al, still. His ancient uncle stared at his beloved nephew, and I saw an expression I had never known. A face drained of life. My father, too, looking at his younger brother by fifteen months, his business partner, the person he loved without reservation, my father was suspended, inanimate, and deadened in life, also.

As Mother lay dying, she was silent. Her last words, spoken four days before to her playful cat, were "Be still." Then no more. At her bedside, for her final breath, an indelible image, I watched as that shocking, awesome moment of death came. No drama is greater. I still see it.

A time came when I regretted having been a good daughter and wished I hadn't spent those eleven years on her. I told a friend, and she was surprised. "But don't you feel good about yourself, because you did it?" I didn't. I felt my sacrifice, if it was, was wasted on her. Now I have to let go of that.

"Attention is the natural prayer of the soul."
—NICOLAS MALEBRANCHE,
seventeenth-century philosopher

On April 23, 2007, *The New Yorker* published a most informative and significant essay on the body, medicine, aging, and doctors. Atul Gawande's "The Way We Age Now" is revelatory.

Here's how it begins: "The hardest substance in the human body is the white enamel of the teeth."

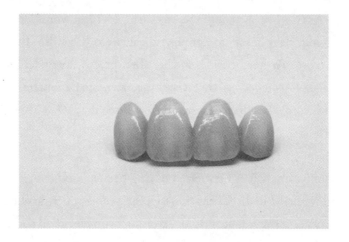

Now, this sentence was the first of many revelations. My periodontist once explained, my mouth wide open, the first place we lose weight is in the gums. I believed faces lost weight first, before the rest of the body, but now I understood why they looked gaunt. That sinking in, caused by thinner gums.

But white enamel—the hardest substance in the body. People needed to eat raw everything. Fire came later.

"With age, [enamel] wears away . . . Meanwhile, the blood supply to the pulp and the roots atrophies, and the flow of the saliva diminishes; the gums tend to become inflamed and pull away from the teeth." And even "scrupulous dental care" doesn't stop what aging will do.

Wear and tear, and genetics, he discusses both theories of aging. And why and how the body ages—the heart thickens, say. Skin dries with age. Blood flow is central.

Geriatric medicine and doctors, he tells us, look differently at aging bodies, and treat the elderly differently. (I glimpsed this in my family's sole meeting with the geriatric psychiatrist Dr. M., who helped us get Mother out of the hospital, home to die with hospice care.)

To me, the most important sentence:

"Most of us in medicine, however, don't know how to think about decline."

Doctors won't have complete success with an elderly person, because no matter what, they decline. Gerontologists seek the best way of treating people in decline. To make their charges more comfortable, less likely to fall, seeing they don't eat alone too often.

I watched Mother have her toenails clipped. They had gotten very hard. A professional—actually, I don't know if he was a podiatrist, nurse, nurse's aide—came to the house. The first time I saw this man at her feet, clipping her nails, I found it strange. You, younger person, can clip your own nails. Then I understood the necessity. What if her nail was cut incorrectly, she got a hangnail, an infection. She was frail. Gawande discusses frailty. The old become frail. You see that in the way they move, the stiffness in their stride. They can come to look brittle, breakable, especially, when they're skinny. A geriatric doctor will want her patients to put on some weight.

Mostly, the elderly are treated by the medical establishment the way they are treated generally in society—as if they have outlasted their welcome, time stamped, get off the shelf. Few want to imagine their decline, and youth doesn't, why should it. The sight of old people is a rude shot into future realities.

One practical thing I did: After Mother died, I contacted a long-term-care provider and signed up David and me. Observing Mother and her many needs, recognizing how much money was needed, I didn't want to waste any more time doing it. Even if you have children and imagine they will help you, they will be burdened, overburdened, and also they might not help you. They might think it's your fault, etc., that you didn't prepare, etc. They might fight among themselves. Or what if you have just one child. Even if you have loads of money, still you don't know how long you'll need care, what special care you might need, and you don't know how long you'll last. Think of Sunny von Bülow, comatose for many years, lying in a room in a hospital. I imagine she didn't have a living will.

The artist Kiki Smith told me, "Life wants to live," a profound encapsulation of what struggle is for. People in the worst of times go on. People live under the most gruesome of conditions. So this fighting to live, this refusal to die, suggested to me when I was a child that death must be awful. But really I shouldn't have inferred that, since death is only not life. Though like most other humans, I resist the future of not being, occasionally telling myself it's just the big sleep. It's what it/I was before I was born. Etc.

I asked Mother, long before she was sick, if she was afraid to die. She said she wasn't. She didn't believe in anything, no afterlife, and she didn't believe she'd join her husband in heaven.

I asked Mother, when ill but lucid: Life is hard, terrible things happen. Do you think life is worth it? Yes, she said, because there are also beautiful things in life. She didn't specify which things, didn't mention love, friendship, walks in the city, opera, children, books, the beauty of the sky. Her answer was unlike anything I'd ever heard her say. Also, I had never asked her a question like it.

I didn't know her. After all, after writing this I can still only speculate. I don't know why she became the person she was. I don't know if she had dark moments of the soul. Or about what.

I wish I had asked her: What do you make of yourself, Sophie Merrill Tillman. But then there are many regrets after a parent dies.

Acknowledgments

To my dear sisters, who had the same mother and a different one and lived through the same difficult eleven years; to the friends who consoled me during those years; to Richard Nash, guide and goad, without whom much of my recent work wouldn't have been published; to Joy Harris, my friend and agent, who keeps faith in me when I don't; to my former editor, Yuka Igarashi, whose acuity and attention were invaluable; to my new editor, Mensah Demary, whose appreciation of this book helped me understand and improve it; to his assistant, Cecilia Flores, whose involvement with *MOTHERCARE* was so helpful and pleasurable; to Wah-Ming Chang, for her excellent eye and sense of everything, and to Andy Hunter who wants me to be happy. And, always, to David, steady beat in life.

© Heather Sten

LYNNE TILLMAN's latest novel is *Men
and Apparitions*. Her essays and stories appear in various literary journals, art catalogs,
and magazines. Tillman has received a Guggenheim Fellowship and an Andy Warhol
Foundation Arts Writers Grant. She lives in
New York with bassist David Hofstra.